T0110432

LAST NIGHT
I DREAMED OF PEACE

The Diary of Dang Thuy Tram

TRANSLATED BY

Andrew X. Pham

INTRODUCTION BY

Frances FitzGerald

NOTES BY

*Jane Barton Griffith, Robert Whitehurst,
and Dang Kim Tram*

LAST NIGHT
I DREAMED OF PEACE

Dang Thuy Tram

THREE RIVERS PRESS
NEW YORK

Translation copyright © 2007 by Andrew X. Pham
Introduction copyright © 2007 by Frances FitzGerald

All rights reserved.
Published in the United States by Three Rivers Press, an imprint of the Crown
Publishing Group, a division of Random House, Inc., New York.
www.crownpublishing.com

THREE RIVERS PRESS and the Tugboat design are registered
trademarks of Random House, Inc.

Originally published in Vietnam as *Nhat Ky Dang Thuy Tram*
by Nha Nam/Nha Xuat Ban Hoi Nha Van in 2005. Copyright © 2005
by Doan Ngoc Tram.
This translation was originally published in hardcover in the United States
by Harmony Books, an imprint of the Crown Publishing Group,
a division of Random House, Inc., New York, in 2007.

Library of Congress Cataloging-in-Publication Data

Dang, Thuy Tram, 1943–1970
[Nhat ky Dang Thuy Tram. English]
Last night I dreamed of peace: the diary of Dang Thuy Tram /
Dang Thuy Tram; translated by Andrew X. Pham; introduction by
Frances FitzGerald; notes by Jane Barton Griffith, Robert
Whitehurst, and Dang Kim Tram.—1st American ed.
1. Dang, Thuy Tram, 1943–1970—Diaries. 2. Vietnam War,
1961–1975—Medical care—Vietnam—Quang Ngai (Province)
3. Physicians—Vietnam—Diaries. I. Title.
DS559.44.D3613 2007
959.704'37—dc22
[B]   2007008201

ISBN 978-0-307-34738-1

Design by Lynne Amft
Map by Mapping Specialists, Ltd., Madison, WI.

First Paperback Edition

146119704

"Operated on one case of appendicitis with inadequate anesthesia. I had only a few meager vials of Novocain to give the soldier, but he never groaned once during the entire procedure. He even smiled to encourage me."

The diary of Dang Thuy Tram begins on April 8, 1968, just two months after the Tet offensive. She is twenty-five years old, the chief physician at a field hospital in the mountains of central Vietnam. It's a civilian clinic, but she treats mainly sick and wounded soldiers. Sometimes large North Vietnamese army, or main force guerrilla, units pass by, leaving as many as eighty patients in her thatched-roof hospital. Sometimes she walks many miles through the rugged mountains or down to the lowlands to care for the wounded on the field of battle. She also trains young people to be health practitioners in Duc Pho, the district she has been assigned to in Quang Ngai Province.

When Thuy arrived from Hanoi the year before, fresh out of medical school, her superiors had hesitated before sending her to the isolated clinic. Small and slight with a pale complexion, she was a city girl who had grown up in relatively privileged circumstances. Her father was a surgeon at St. Paul's Hospital, her mother a lecturer at the Hanoi School of Pharmacology and one of the leading experts on the use of Vietnamese medicinal plants. Her parents weren't rich—no one was in North Vietnam at the time—but they were cultured people who filled their small house on Giang Vo Street in Hanoi with books and flowers. Her father played Western classical music to relax after surgery and taught Thuy to play the violin and the guitar.

The eldest of five children—four girls and much younger boy—Thuy Tram attended the elite Chu Van An high school. Founded by the French in 1906 as the Lycée du Protectorate, the school with its campus on the West Lake had trained generations of prominent Vietnamese intellectuals, artists, and politicians. For four years Thuy, dressed in a white ao dai, studied in the handsome French colonial buildings with their spacious classrooms, the breeze coming through the transoms over the high louvered doorways. Her concentration was science, but she loved literature— Vietnamese poetry and the French and Russian novels sent from the Soviet Union. According to classmates, she was beautiful, intelligent, and warm-hearted, and all the boys were a little in love with her. She went on to Hanoi University Medical School and, following in her father's footsteps, trained as a surgeon. On graduating, she was accepted for advance study in optical surgery, but she chose instead to serve in the war zone of the South.

On December 23, 1966, she boarded a truck in Hanoi with a group of civilians—journalists, photographers, and doctors—and drove 250 miles south to a staging area in Quang Binh Province. From there, she and her companions set off on foot with heavy packs on their backs and walked for three months down what the Americans called the Ho Chi Minh Trail through the mountains of the Troung Son range. Their destination was Quang Ngai, the fifth province below the demilitarized zone that divided the North from the South, and they reached it in late March or early April.

Like the other provinces of central Vietnam, Quang Ngai has a dramatic topography: high mountains with rivers that plunge down through foothills to a coastal plain and into the China Sea. In Quang Ngai, the plain is eighty kilometers long and ten to twenty-five kilometers wide, well irrigated by tributary streams and extremely fertile. The Vietnamese are rice growers, and when the first settlers came down from the North after the conquest of the Kingdom of Champa in the fifteenth century, they turned their backs to the mountains and built their villages on the plain. In central Vietnam, the villages are composed of widely dispersed hamlets, and in the early 1960s, before the arrival of the American troops, the hamlets of Quang Ngai nestled within bamboo hedges and groves of trees, looking over their paddy fields, emerald green in the spring. In some, the dwellings were made of clay and thatch, but others had fine houses with huge polished beams holding up the red-tiled roofs, brick courtyards where the rice was threshed, and outbuildings for pigs, chickens, and water buffalo. At the time, the province was almost entirely rural. Each district had a small market town with open-fronted shops lining its main street, but even its capital, Quang Ngai City, was only a town with a few government buildings. Still, Route One, the main north-south highway, bisected the plain, and all the roads were busy with trucks, donkey carts, and young people on bikes going to and from high school—the boys in clean shirts, the girls in their ao dais.

For all of its bucolic looks, the province was a guerrilla stronghold. It had belonged to what the villagers called "the Resistance," or "the Liberation," for decades. In 1930 one of the first peasant revolts against French rule erupted in the province, and after World War II it became a center of revolutionary activity. In 1945 a communist uprising in the province heralded Ho Chi Minh's declaration of Vietnam's independence and the formation of the

Democratic Republic of Vietnam in Hanoi. Thereafter, the Viet Minh, the anti-colonial predecessor of the National Liberation Front (the Viet Cong), so dominated the province that the French troops never penetrated it in force. When, after the end of the French war in 1954, the United States installed a non-communist government in Saigon and made the demilitarized zone into a political boundary, it in essence cut off Quang Ngai and its neighboring provinces from the government they had helped to create. In the late 1950s and early 1960s, the regime in Saigon made various attempts to bring its rebellious provinces under control, but all of them failed. In Quang Ngai, the influence of the Saigon government never reached beyond a few of the larger towns. By the time the first regular American troops arrived there in 1965, a whole generation of young people in the rural areas had grown up, as Thuy had, in the revolution.

Thuy had spent some of 1967 on the coastal plain of Quang Ngai, working in the villages of Duc Pho. She felt at home on the plain there in a way she never did in the mountains. "I miss the lowlands, covered with green rice fields, thick with grain-heavy stalks, dotted with colored dresses and the white hats of pretty girls," she wrote. The mountains were foreign territory to her, as they were to most Vietnamese. In Duc Pho District—the southernmost district in the province—there were Vietnamese villages in the foothills, but above them, the only settlements were those of the hill tribes, peoples ethnically and culturally different from the Vietnamese, who practiced swidden, or slash-and-burn, agriculture. Apart from the clearings these highlanders had made, there was nothing but forest—a forest of thick bush twenty to thirty feet high with trails that ran through it like tunnels. Thuy's clinic was hidden away in the brush near a river. The clinic was invisible from the air, but there was an American firebase at the top of the mountain, and an exposed cooking fire or the noise of troop movements could always give away its location. The clinic Thuy had been first assigned to had been destroyed by bombing just before she arrived. It was bleak in the mountains and cold in autumn and winter, and when she wasn't busy with patients, Thuy had to help cut firewood, dig shelters, and haul rice sacks. Sometimes army units would bring dozens of patients with serious wounds, and she would have to work through the night, making diagnoses and performing operations without electricity. The soldiers would stay for a while, then move on, leaving the clinic with only the dead and the dying. Then Thuy would have time for reflection.

Thuy began keeping a diary when she left Hanoi for the South. Unfortunately, her first diary has not survived, so the book begins a year after her arrival in Quang Ngai, at a time when she was desperately unhappy.

Thuy had gone to the South out of patriotism but also because of the man she calls M., whom she had loved since the age of sixteen. M., whose real name was Khuong The Hung but who used the pen name Do Moc, came from another intellectual Hanoi family, and his parents were close friends of Thuy's. Handsome and intelligent, he wrote poetry and composed music. A match between them would have been entirely suitable, and he courted her in her college and medical school days. But he was six years older than she was, and in 1962 he left and worked for a while with a troupe of singers and actors, then joined the guerrillas in central Vietnam. He wrote her letters, and on her graduation five years later, Thuy, "following the call of country and love," set out for

Quang Ngai, hoping to see him from time to time. By then, M. had become the captain and chief political officer of an NLF sapper group, which had earned a reputation for heroism. Because of the loss of Thuy's first diary, it's unclear what happened between the two of them, but by April 1968, Thuy understood that he didn't love her in the pure, bright way that she loved him. Was it that he had dedicated himself entirely to the struggle and assumed he would die in it? Or was it that he had had affairs with other women? Or both? She had her pride, but to her he represented all her hopes and dreams of happiness, and she couldn't bear to give them up—certainly not amid all the hardships and dangers she was experiencing. "Oh, why was I born a dreamy girl demanding so much of life?" she asks herself plaintively.

Thuy had an enormous capacity—and an enormous need—for love and affection. Many of the young soldiers who came through the clinic fell in love with the kind and attractive doctor, and she developed strong attachments to some of them, as well as to some of her female co-workers. Thuy often worried that her relationships with these men would be seen as sexual or romantic, inappropriate for someone in her position. They were certainly not sexual, and none of the young men ever occupied the space in her life that M. did. Yet the emotional bonds formed in wartime run deep. Some of the soldiers she adopted as "brothers," and some she grew to love and depend on in a way she couldn't depend on M. When they died, as many of them did, she felt she had lost a member of her family. She was desolate.

Another theme in the early part of the diaries is Thuy's frustration with the local branch of the Communist Party. The Party was something sacred to her, as it was to many in the resistance. Ho Chi

Minh's party, unlike Stalin's or Mao's, put an emphasis on personal virtue, and its cadre were called upon to represent revolutionary ideals. Membership in the Party was also of great practical consequence to Thuy, since it was the leadership and the local branch made the decisions in her district. She thought she should have been made a member, but the invitation did not come immediately. Thuy suspected that some of the cadre were simply jealous of her. They labeled her a "bourgeois," and she had to admit that she was one, though she could not accept the idea that that made her ipso facto inferior to all working-class people. What she doesn't say is that most, if not all, of the people she worked with were country people with nowhere near her level of education. That she made so many close friends—and was eventually taken into the Party—was a tribute to her generous nature and her ability to adapt.

In her diaries Thuy often gives herself advice. "Oh, Thuy! Overcome these pains in your heart. Be joyful . . . You cannot live with sentiments alone, you must also possess a will. Do you understand that, you stubborn girl? . . . Twenty-five years old already, be steady and mature with that age." Whatever role these admonitions played, Thuy did grow and mature in the two years the diary covers. Among other things, she comes to see herself and others more clearly, to trust her own judgment and to take satisfaction from her accomplishments. "What am I?" she asks. "I am a girl with a heart brimming over with emotions, yet with a mind that never falters before a complex and dangerous situation." This was exactly the case, as we discover in the second half of the book, when the American forces close in on the guerrilla bases throughout Duc Pho.

In the late spring of 1965, two months after the first American combat troops arrived in Vietnam, the 3rd Marine Amphibious Force was dispatched to Quang Ngai, where it began an assault on NVA and guerrilla forces in the region. It remained there until April 1967, when General William Westmoreland, the commander of U.S. forces in Vietnam, created Task Force Oregon, a group of three Army brigades, to replace it. In Quang Ngai, the American troops faced a formidable foe: in addition to the North Vietnamese divisions that operated in central Vietnam, there were three main force guerrilla battalions in the province and guerrilla units in almost every village and hamlet. The roads were mined and booby-trapped; the American patrols were ambushed, and their bases were often mortared or attacked by sappers. Unable to find the guerrillas amid the population that supported them, the American forces used their overwhelming firepower against the villages. As a matter of policy, the Marines bombed and shelled the hamlets from which they took fire and the hamlets they believed were contributing food or labor to the enemy. "The U.S. Marines will not hesitate to destroy immediately any village or hamlet harboring the Viet Cong," one leaflet dropped on the villages read.

By August 1967, according to Jonathan Schell, the Marines and the Army units that succeeded them had destroyed 70 percent of the hamlets on the coastal plain, caused countless civilian casualties, and driven some 40 percent of the 650,000 people in the province into towns and refugee camps along Route One. By then, the U.S. command had come to see the "generation of refugees" not just as an unavoidable consequence of military operations but as a means of depriving the guerrillas of the population they needed for support. At a press conference that fall, Robert Komer, the chief of the U.S. pacification program in Vietnam, explained, "If we can attrit the population base of the Viet Cong, it will accelerate the process of degrading the V.C."

In Duc Pho District, where the 3rd Brigade of the 4th Infantry Division was based that August, almost half of the population of 100,000 had been driven into towns or refugee camps. Some of the hamlets along Route One remained standing, but much of the district had become a free fire zone where people lived in caves or in tunnels that also served as bunkers for the guerrillas. Many of the hamlets had been burned or bulldozed to deny the guerrillas shelter; the fields were pockmarked with craters, and the nearby forests defoliated. (In three and a half months the 3rd Brigade's battery had fired 64,000 artillery shells on Duc Pho and the adjoining district.) From April to August the brigade had—by its account—killed 1,875 enemy combatants and captured 566 firearms. But in a series of small engagements over those months, the brigade had itself suffered many casualties. In a force of 800 combat troops directly exposed to enemy fire, 120 had been killed and 490 wounded.

In September, Task Force Oregon was reconstituted with different units as the Americal Division; from then until November 1971, it operated in Quang Ngai as well as in the province of Quang Tin to the north. The Americal eventually became known as the worst division in the American army. Its three unrelated brigades never fully cohered, and other units were often transferred in or out of it. The 11th Light Infantry Brigade, based in Duc Pho, was a particularly troubled unit. It went into action without combat training, with few veteran officers or NCOs and a great many raw recruits. Morale, never high in the first place, deteriorated as the casualties mounted; its base in Duc Pho became rife with racial tensions and hostilities between draftees and "lifers." Colin Powell, who as a major served in a battalion of the 11th Infantry for three months in 1968, later wrote that he moved his cot around every night at the base "partly to thwart Viet Cong informants who might be tracking me, but also because I did not rule out attacks on authority from within the battalion itself." On March 16, 1968, a platoon from the 11th entered the village of Son My in northern Quang Ngai, herded the old men, women, and children into a ditch, and shot 504 of them. The incident, covered up for more than a year, became known as the My Lai massacre. Still, the 11th, and Americal as a whole, fought much the same war as their predecessors. The NVA and the guerrillas responded aggressively, and in early 1969 they launched coordinated attacks on all the Americal's bases. But the cumulative effect of the bombing and shelling took its toll.

Thuy describes this war vividly. She watched jets on bombing runs, gunships firing streams of bullets and tracers, helicopter assaults, and sweeps by the American forces. She notes how the defoliant Agent Orange debilitated herself and her fellow cadre, and how a white phosphorus shell roasted a man's body. She saw hamlets that had just been bulldozed and the survivors wandering around through the devastation, unwilling to leave their homes. On a night emergency mission, she walked across the national highway and through hills so bright with lights and flares she felt herself on a stage. Another night she walked through an area she calls Khe Sanh, the rice bowl of Duc Pho District, which the Americans guarded with artillery, constant patrols, and an electronic surveillance system. She slept in underground shelters, spent a night up to her chest in water, and was almost killed many times.

On April 2, 1969, the American troops assaulted a hamlet near her clinic, forcing the patients and staff to abandon the compound. From then on, she and her co-workers were constantly on the move, unable to find a safe place for the clinic. Some of their temporary quarters were bombed, others discovered by enemy troops. When they moved, most of the soldiers and nurses would go ahead with the ambulatory patients, leaving Thuy and a few others with the severely injured until they could come back with stretchers. On one occasion, the troops came so close that she and another young woman had to drag a heavy man with a broken leg into a hole. On another, she had to flee without her backpack that contained most of her possessions.

On June 2, 1970, her temporary clinic in the Nai Sang Mountains was bombed, and five people were killed. When it was bombed again on the twelfth, the cadre assumed—correctly, as it turned out—that an informer had given away their position. The next day everyone left except for Thuy, three female medics, and five seriously wounded men. Even the Party cadre for the clinic wouldn't stay with them. After that, Thuy watched for the enemy troops every day and asked herself if she would have the heart to leave the wounded if they came. A week went by, and still no one came back for them. On June 20, with only rice enough left for the evening meal, Thuy, wondering if they had been abandoned, sent two of the young women out to find help. Her diary ends there. The American troops returned, and several days later she was found by a highlander of the local H're people, dead with a bullet through her forehead.

Those who read Thuy's diaries before the publication of this book supposed that Thuy's co-workers had deserted her, and that she died defending her patients. The after-action report of the American company, just recently brought to light, however, shows that the clinic had been resupplied by the time of her death, and that the injured soldiers were evacuated. Thuy was shot while walking down a trail with an NVA soldier and two other people. She had not been left to die with her patients.

The Diaries

In April 2005, as Hanoi was preparing to celebrate the thirtieth anniversary of the liberation of the South, a package arrived for Thuy's mother, Doan Ngoc Tram, containing the diaries.

The package, delivered by an American visiting Hanoi, had been sent by Fred Whitehurst, a lawyer who had served with a military intelligence detachment at the American's base in Duc Pho. In 1970, Whitehurst's duties had included taking a last look through the accumulated captured documents and destroying those of no military value. One day, he was throwing documents into a fire in a 55-gallon drum, when his interpreter, Sergeant Nguyen Trung Hieu, said over his shoulder, "Don't burn this one, Fred. It has fire in it already." Startled, Whitehurst saved the document—a collection of pages sewn together with a cardboard cover, no bigger than a pack of cigarettes. He later saved a second diary that was brought to the base after Thuy's death. In the evenings Hieu read him passages from the diary. The son of a naval officer, and a volunteer for Vietnam, Whitehurst was a gung-ho soldier, but Thuy's diaries moved him deeply. "Human to human, I fell in love with her," he later said. Against regulations, he took the diaries home with him when he left in 1972, after serving three tours in Vietnam.

The diaries went into his filing cabinet and stayed there while he took a doctorate in chemistry and joined the FBI as a forensic scientist, an expert on explosives residue. Whitehurst often thought of trying to return them to Thuy's family, but he had no idea how to find the family, and as an FBI agent, he could hardly approach officials in the Vietnamese embassy. In the mid-1990s he became a celebrated whistle-blower, exposing corruption and incompetence in FBI investigations, notably that of the 1993 World Trade Center bombing. After a bitter fight with the agency, he quit and began to think about the diaries again. Hoping that he might find Thuy's family if the diaries were published, he gave them to his brother Rob, another Vietnam vet, who had married a southern Vietnamese woman and spoke Vietnamese. Rob began translating them in his spare time, and soon became as obsessed as Fred was with Thuy's story and with the idea of returning them to Vietnam. In March 2005, the two brothers took the diaries to a conference on the Vietnam War at Texas Tech University, where they met an Air Force veteran who was traveling to Hanoi the following month. They gave him a copy of the diaries, and he located Thuy's family with the help of an employee of a Quaker group in Hanoi.

Thuy's father and brother had died by that time—her father had had a paralytic stroke when he heard of Thuy's death—but her mother was a lively eighty-one-year-old, and her three sisters had families and professional careers. Rob struck up an e-mail conversation with the youngest sister, Kim Tram, who worked as an engineer and in her spare time translated English-language children's books into Vietnamese. Rob and Fred were adopted into Thuy's family as "sons" and "brothers," and in August they went to Hanoi to meet the family. To their amazement, they had become celebrities. Dozens of people, among them journalists, came to greet them at the airport; later, they were interviewed on television and welcomed by Vietnamese officials, among them the prime minister, Phan Van Kai.

Thuy's diaries were published in Hanoi on July 18, 2005. To the surprise of the book publisher, they caused an immediate sensation. By the time the Whitehursts arrived, twenty thousand copies were in print, the diaries had been excerpted in a newspaper, and a television film about Dang Thuy Tram was in preparation. A year and half later, they had sold 430,000 copies—this in a country where few books sell more than 5,000 copies. The diaries struck a particular chord among young readers. Two-thirds of all Vietnamese were born after 1975, and for them the war was ancient history, and a history that was taught in a dry, stylized fashion. Other war diaries had been published, but, like the textbooks, they spoke mainly of heroism and great victories. Thuy's diaries broke the mold. Here was a brave, idealistic young woman, but one with vulnerabilities and self-doubts: a romantic in spite of all her discipline. Her descriptions of the pathos of the soldiers, as well as of their heroism, reminded readers that those who had died for their cause were people much like themselves. Furthermore, the government, which had previously censored novels about the horrors of war, seemed to understand that the diaries brought the war to life for the young in a way that the old rhetoric of invincibility did not.

On a second trip to Vietnam in the spring of 2006, Rob Whitehurst found that hundreds of people had visited Thuy's grave in a cemetery on the outskirts of Hanoi. In Duc Pho, ground had been broken for the Dang Thuy Tram hospital, and a memorial marked the place where she had died in the mountains. She had become a folk hero. On his trips to Duc Pho, Rob met a number of the people she had written about in her diary, among them Sang, whom she had operated on for a stomach infection; Khiem, whom she had dragged to safety, and who now thanked her every day for operating on his leg and saving it from amputation. Thuong, her beloved Thuong, had been captured and sent to a prisoner-of-war camp, but had been released in the prisoner exchange of 1973. Two years later he returned to Quang Ngai, and, finding that Thuy was dead, located her grave and later helped her family to find it. Thuan had been killed in 1971 by an ARVN patrol; Tan, the Party cadre she was so fond of, was dead by then, but he had survived the war, married his girlfriend, and named his daughter Thuy Tram.

As for M., he remains something of a mystery. He survived the war, married, and had two sons. According to a friend of his, he had told Thuy in 1967 that he had devoted his life to the war, that he did not expect to survive it, and that therefore he could only be a brother to her. This is plausible and consistent with some of Thuy's account, but his friend adds that the war had changed him and that with more than twenty wounds on his body, he didn't think he deserved to marry Thuy. Possibly this was the case, but when he returned to Hanoi after the war, he didn't go see Thuy's mother: an indication that he felt guilty about the way he had treated her. He died in 1999, so we will never know the full story, but in a way that neither could have imagined, it's her light that shines on him.

FRANCES FITZGERALD

A Note on the Translation

This translation required considerable sensitivity to the spirit of the author's words as well as to the conditions in which she committed them to her diaries. It is a responsibility that extends beyond the translator to every reader.

Dr. Thuy Tram wrote her diaries under extreme duress. She penned these entries in battle trenches, bomb shelters, and triages, and in wards filled with dying patients. Through destruction, hunger, extreme fatigue, loneliness, and psychological trauma, this remarkable young woman still had the presence to reach for the literary and the sublime.

Her writing leaped nimbly from prose to poetry, from meditation to self-examination, from confession to reflection. In some places she talked to herself. In others she held conversations with absent friends. She switched viewpoints frequently, from the first to the second to the third person, with ease and without warning. The reader will find it helpful to keep in mind that she wrote in the flowery literary style of her era; she was innocent in the ways of the heart, an inexperienced romantic; and she died without knowing anything more intimate than kisses. Such were the traditional values of her generation.

Regardless of how the diaries are read or perceived, there are three undeniable truths about the author. First, her heart was noble. Second, her life was guided by ideals. Third, her sacrifice was as tragic as it was heroic.

In such a raw composition, the things left unsaid are as telling as those articulated.

I could not have made this translation without my father, Thong Van Pham. He was born in Tong Xuyen and grew up in Hanoi, not far from where Tram lived with her family. His background and knowledge of the language and culture of that time were vital to the translation of the diaries. It took us approximately five months working closely in tandem to complete the translation.

Although my father's modesty and "old world" sensibilities make him decline to be acknowledged as co-translator, it is obvious that he did half of the work. It is also clear to me that I could not have adequately translated a single passage without him. Certainly, neither of us would have dared to tackle this project alone.

I would like to thank my wonderful agent, Jandy Nelson, for her acumen and friendship, and my editor, John Glusman, for his confidence and support.

Most of all, I would like to express our gratitude to Kim Tram for her generous assistance and guidance. We would have erred in many instances without her involvement. Kim Tram's comprehensive understanding of the diaries gave us substantial confidence in approaching the text. We are deeply indebted.

We would also like to thank the Tram family for permitting us the honor of participating in the preservation of Dr. Thuy Tram's legacy.

ANDREW X. PHAM

CHRONOLOGY

1945

AUGUST 19: The August Revolution. The Viet Minh enter Hanoi.
SEPTEMBER 2: Ho Chi Minh proclaims Vietnam's independence and the establishment of the Democratic Republic of Vietnam.

1946

DECEMBER: The French-Indochina war begins.

1954

MAY 8: The French garrison at Dien Bien Phu falls to the Viet Minh.
JULY 20-21: An international conference in Geneva creates a provisional demarcation line at the 17th parallel that divides Vietnam pending a political settlement to be achieved by nationwide elections before July 1956. The French-supported government of the Emperor Bao Dai denounces the agreements.

1955

In Saigon, Bao Dai's prime minister, Ngo Dinh Diem, defeats Bao Dai in a referendum and becomes president of the Republic of Vietnam. He rejects the Geneva Agreements and refuses to participate in a nationwide election, a decision backed by the United States.

1956

Diem begins a crackdown on the Viet Minh and other dissidents in the South; insurgent activity begins the following year.

1960

The National Liberation Front (NLF) is formed by communists in the South. The Saigon regime calls its members the "Viet Cong," for Vietnamese communists, though the Front includes many non-communists. North Vietnam begins infiltrating cadres and weapons into the South via the Ho Chi Minh Trail.

1965

FEBRUARY 24: The United States begins a sustained bombing of North Vietnam.

MARCH 8: The first American combat troops arrive in Vietnam. They number 500,000 by the end of 1967.

1968

JANUARY 31: North Vietnamese and Viet Cong troops launch the Tet offensive, attacking towns and cities throughout South Vietnam.

MARCH 31: President Lyndon Johnson calls a partial halt to the bombing of the North, agrees to negotiations with Hanoi, and announces he will not run for reelection.

MAY: Peace negotiations between the United States and the Democratic Republic of Vietnam begin in Paris.

1969

JANUARY: The Paris peace talks expand to include the Republic of Vietnam and the recently formed Provisional Revolutionary Government representing the Viet Cong.

MARCH 18: President Richard Nixon begins the secret bombing of Cambodia.

JUNE 8: Nixon announces the first in a series of U.S. troop withdrawals from Vietnam.

SEPTEMBER 3: Ho Chi Minh dies in Hanoi.

1973

JANUARY 27: The Paris Peace Agreement is completed and signed.

MARCH 29: The last American combat troops leave South Vietnam, and prisoners of war are exchanged. But the cease-fire does not last.

1975

North Vietnamese troops begin a major offensive in early March. On April 30 they take Saigon, and the war is over.

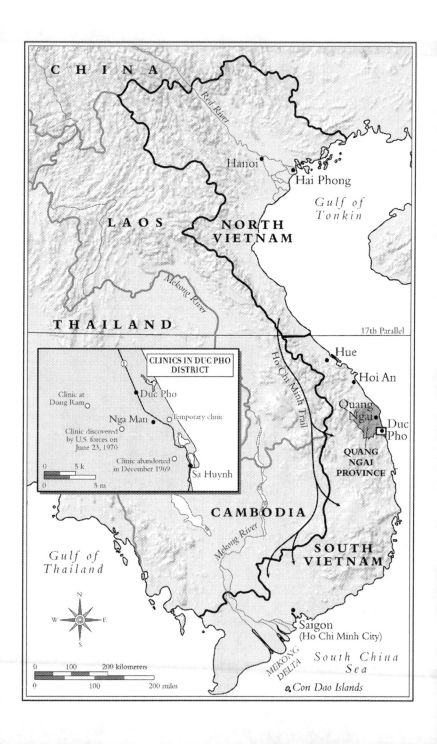

CHINA

Red River

Hanoi

Hai Phong

Gulf of
Tonkin

LAOS

NORTH
VIETNAM

Mekong River

THAILAND

17th Parallel

Hue

Ho Chi Minh Trail

Hoi An

Quang
Ngai

Duc
Pho

QUANG
NGAI
PROVINCE

CLINICS IN DUC PHO DISTRICT

Clinic at
Dong Ram

Duc Pho

Nga Man   Temporary clinic

Clinic discovered
by U.S. forces on
June 23, 1970

Clinic abandoned
in December 1969

Sa Huynh

0   5 k

0   5 m

CAMBODIA

Mekong River

SOUTH
VIETNAM

Gulf of
Thailand

N

W   E

S

Saigon
(Ho Chi Minh City)

South China
Sea

0   100   200 kilometers

0   100   200 miles

MEKONG
DELTA

Con Dao Islands

BOOK I

1968 - 1969

The inflamed days
Joy, sadness condensing in my heart

Đặng Thùy Trâm

A person's most valuable possession is life. We only live once; we must live so as not to sorely regret the months and years lived wastefully, not to be ashamed of the months and years lived wastefully, so that when we die we can say, "All my life and all my strength have been dedicated to the most noble goal in life, the struggle to liberate the human race."

N. A. OSTROVSKY[1]

To live is to face the storms and not to cower before them.

---

[1] From *How the Steel Was Tempered,* a popular Russian novel by Nikolai Ostrovsky (1904–1936). Widely read in socialist and communist countries, it describes how courage and self-sacrifice can overcome obstacles to build a new society that will not exploit the working class.

8 April 1968

Operated on one case of appendicitis with inadequate anesthesia. I had only a few meager vials of Novocain to give the soldier, but he never groaned once during the entire procedure. He even smiled to encourage me. Seeing that forced smile on lips withered by exhaustion, I empathized with him immensely.

Even though his appendix had not ruptured, I was very sorry to find an infection in his abdomen. After a fruitless hour of searching for the cause, I could only treat him with antibiotics, insert a catheter, and close the wound. A whirl of emotions unsettled me: a physician's concerns and a comrade's compassion and admiration for this soldier.

Brushing the stray hair back from his forehead, I wanted to say, "If I cannot even heal people like you, this sorrow will not fade from my medical career."

10 April 1968

It is finished. You have all gone this afternoon, leaving us in an empty jungle with only our intense yearning, this loss of you.[2] You

---

[2]North Vietnam and the southern resistance fighters, the National Front for the Liberation of South Vietnam (NLF), transported supplies not only via the Truong Son Mountain trail (known

have gone, but this place holds your shadows: the pathways, the pretty benches, the echoes of your impassioned poems.

"Everybody put on your pack. Let's go."

At Brother Tuan's[3] order, you shouldered your crude rucksacks made from salvaged American bags. All was ready, but each of you still lingered, waiting your turn to shake my hand for the last time. Suddenly a strange longing for the North surged through me like a stormy river and . . . I cried so hard I could not face all your farewells.

No, be on your way brothers! I'll see you again one day in our beloved North.

For a night and a day, I worried about Sang's[4] operation. I was so happy to see him sit up this afternoon. His face bore deep lines of pain and fatigue, but a smile slowly bloomed on his fragile lips when he saw me. His hands cupped over mine, a touch filled with warmth and trust.

Oh, you young, brave wounded soldier, my love for you is as vast as it is deep: it's a physician's compassion for her patient; it's a sister's love for her sick brother (we're the same age, you and I); and in admiration, it is a love special beyond others.

---

as the Ho Chi Minh Trail), but also used the South China Sea route along the coast of Vietnam, called the Ho Chi Minh Sea Route. This effort to move supplies by sea was referred to by the code name Market Time. The boats, usually trawlers, were falsely registered as fishing vessels and took supplies into all the coastal areas of the central and southern parts of Vietnam, including the Mekong Delta. In 1968 the U.S. military attacked one of these large boats, known as Boat 43. Some of the crew survived and were brought to Thuy's clinic. The 10 April diary entry marks the day Thuy said good-bye to this group of young men.

[3]Tran van Tuan was party branch secretary on Boat 43.

[4]Thuy's abdominal operation on Huynh Doan Sang saved Sang's life. Three years older than Thuy, Sang is currently sixty-seven years old. After the war, he received a law degree and became chief of Duc Pho's people's procurecy. He now works in his family's noodle shop in Duc Pho, Quang Ngai Province.

Did you see it in my anxious glance? Did you feel the tenderness in my hand on your wound, on your pale, thin arms? I wish you a quick recovery, San, so you can return to your comrades, return to your lonely old mother, who waits for you every hour, every minute.

12 April 1968

Afternoon in the forest, the rain has left the leaves wet and fragile, pale and lucid in the sunbeams, these emerald hands of a maiden imprisoned within a forbidden fortress. The air has gone somberly sad. In the patient ward, silence broods. Murmurs of Huong's[5] conversation drift from the staff's room.

An immense longing envelops me.

Whom do I miss?

Dad, Mom, people who left . . . and a patient waiting for me to come to him.

Within this longing roosts a secret and profound sorrow, silent as this air, heavy as this earth. I feel the wound in my heart still bleeds, an excruciating pain that neither work nor memories can numb.

Oh, let's forget it, Thuy![6]

Forget it for a new hope, something greener, healthier. Take your pride to forget despair. That person does not deserve your pure and faithful love.

---

[5]Nguyen Thi Minh Huong, nurse, died on April 22, 1968.

[6]Many middle- and upper-class Vietnamese have the habit of combining their child's middle name with his first name to form a compound first name. This is particularly common with daughters. It is also common for Vietnamese to give all their children the same first name. For example, "Thuy" in "Dang Thuy Tram" is the middle name, but "Thuy Tram" is also used as her compound first name by her family and friends to distinguish her from her other sisters Dang Phuong Tram, Dang Hien Tram, and Dang Kim Tram. Furthermore, the compound first name can be too long to use regularly, so Vietnamese simply use the middle name. This is not considered a nickname because Vietnamese nicknames tend to be derogatory in nature.

Oh, my dearest ones in this land of Duc Pho, can anyone see my heart? The heart of a lonely girl filled with unanswered hopes and dreams.

13 April 1968

So many letters come from all over. Thank you all for showering me with such warm affection. I read your letters with both joy and sadness.

Why can everyone else love me so, but the man who has my faithful heart cannot?

Isn't that sad, M.?[7]

I want to fill the emptiness in my soul with the affection within these kind letters, but it is impossible. My heart beats stubbornly with the tempo of a twenty-year-old, full of love and affection. Oh, be calm my heart, seek the peaceful rhythm of the sea on a windless afternoon.

14 April 1968

A wounded soldier under my care wrote me a poem. He was sincere in his admiration for my dedication. The poem was filled with compassion for my broken heart, it spoke of the bitter grief of a girl betrayed by her lover.

---

[7] M. was Khuong The Hung, Thuy's unnamed romantic interest, who used the pen name Do Moc. Thuy was in love with M. from her late teens through her college and medical school days. Six years older than Thuy, M. joined the North Vietnamese Army and was assigned to Quang Ngai Province in the central coastal area, which was under the control of the Republic of South Vietnam and the U.S. military forces. Five years after he went south to serve as captain of a commando battalion, Thuy followed him. Whenever Thuy mentions "that soldier" or "that liberation soldier," or "the soldier with the black eyes," she is speaking of M.

Reading his words . . . I am dismayed. I can't help but return the poem with a note beneath it: "Thanks for your loving sympathy, but it seems you don't understand Tram yet. I promise someday I will let you know this woman of SOCIALISM."

Oh! This is the saddest part of my relationship with M. Everyone blames M. and sympathizes with me. But it hurts to know they pity me! I don't care whether it is Thiet, Hao, Nghinh,[8] or anyone else who wants to give me his sympathy, I don't want it.

I can overcome my sorrows alone. I have the will to bury nine years of hope—my soul is still fertile, still strong enough for a beautiful season of flowers yet.

Oh, friends, please don't water this soil with tears of pity. The blooms to come should be nurtured with only freshness and pureness.

M. has made my love for him fade with each passing day. A distance grows between us.

That person doesn't deserve me, does he?

15 April 1968

At noon, the jungle sleeps beneath a thick blanket of silence. I hear San is sick, so I come to his ward. All patients in the room are sleeping, including San. Not wanting to wake him, I tiptoe out, but San's moan pulls me back. He smiles uneasily. . . . He is not sick; perhaps he just wants to see me. I've been busy all day. We haven't talked about his wound.

San asks me, "This was the day you came to Duc Pho, wasn't it?"

---

[8] These three crew members of Boat 43 were being treated at Thuy's clinic.

A full year exactly, San.

I am surprised by his question. I want to sit down and tell San the whole story of the past year, a year of hardships in San's homeland, worthy of pride, but I find it hard to begin. My work means nothing compared to San's or to that of the people of Duc Pho who have fought courageously for twenty years. And it's even sillier to talk with San about how much I miss my family.

San's mother is old. San's father died when she was only twenty-two years old. A young widow, she did not remarry, sacrificing her youth to raise San until he joined the army at nineteen. Five years of flirting with death, and he is still alive.

A month ago, the enemy attacked his unit. San escaped their claws. Fifteen of his comrades sacrificed their lives. But for a twist of fate, he could easily have fallen like the rest at the foot of Portal Mountain[9]; and then, even if San's mother shed all her tears, her son would never come back.

Today they bring San to me. I can never let Death rob this precious son from his mother. She has pinned all her hopes on her precious only son. Never! I must do my best for San as well as for other patients![10] Isn't that a physician's proud duty?

---

[9]Portal Mountain is east of Duc Pho near the coast, and is known as Nui Cua in Vietnamese.

[10]Thuy was assigned to work for the National Liberation Front's public health division and was asked to establish a program to train students in public health methodology and a clinic where both soldiers and civilians could be treated. Seeking a broad national base, the Communist Party created the National Liberation Front as an umbrella political "front" in South Vietnam composed of mainly non-communist groups ranging from religious to women's organizations. At this point in the diary, Thuy is not yet a member of the Communist Party. The guerrilla fighters who fought for the NLF were called "liberation fighters," though the Republic of Vietnam referred to them as "Viet Cong" (Vietnamese Communists) in order to suggest that supporters of the NLF were all communists and not a popular, national movement. American forces typically referred to the guerrilla soldiers as "VC" (Victor Charlie) or "Charlie," which comes from the U.S. Armed Forces' phonetic alphabet.

Van sent me a letter and a gift. How I love Van! Her life is full of sorrows—sorrows that a kind person like Van should never have to bear. She lives with altruism and hopes, and carries the firm convictions of a true revolutionist. There must be compensations for that. Why does life always bring her misfortunes?

I must assume this responsibility; I must bring her hope and joy.

17 April 1968

I said good-bye to Ky and Phuong.[11] After a whole year living together, I finally understood how much they love me today.

Late at night after the farewell party, Ky came to my room. Neither of us knew what to say. He sat with the notebook open, pen in hand, and scribbled meaningless lines.

There was little time. There were many important things you needed to say and write, but why did you keep your silence, my brother? Were you imparting your feelings to me through your red, sleepless eyes, or through your dark, sad smile, the lines on your thin, pale face? He took me in his wiry arms, a brotherly embrace that moved me so much.

When he left, I accompanied him to the stream. Melancholic, I walked back slowly and found the memo he had left for Lien.[12] A

---

[11]Nguyen Thanh Ky and Mai Thuy Phuong were medical specialists.

[12]Tran Thi My Lien was a nurse at the clinic and a close friend of Thuy's. Lien is often mentioned in Thuy's diaries between April of 1968 and July of 1969, when she was killed. Thuy continued to reflect on Lien's death in her diary.

few short lines: "You and Tram must love each other sincerely. Tram came here alone, far away from her family, she has only friends. . . ."

Oh, brother Ky, thank you. I will never forget your love.

And the last night, lying in sister Phuong's comforting arms, I listened to her advice and kept quiet, but I could not stop the hot tears rolling down my face and spilling onto hers.

Oh, sister, I'm still not a Party member today.

22 April 1968

Oh, Huong! Huong died? The news stuns me like a nightmare. One comrade falls down today, another tomorrow. Will these pains ever end? Heaps of flesh and bones keep piling up into a mountain of hatred rising ever taller in our hearts. When? When and when comrades? When can we chase the entire bloodthirsty mob from our motherland?

It's over, our nights of heart-to-heart will never happen again. I can still hear Huong's soothing voice encouraging me, praising me for the faithfulness of my love. It's over, the baths in the stream, the times we shared sweet desserts. Suddenly I remember the day we met by the stream at Nghia Hanh[13]: Huong embraced me, kissed my hair, kissed my cheek while tears of joy came to our eyes.

I feel a stinging stab in my belly when I see Uncle Cong,[14] still calm and unaware of the tragic news that will strike him like a

---

[13]Nghia Hanh District is in Quang Ngai Province.

[14]Uncle Cong is the father of Nguyen Thi Minh Huong.

lightning bolt. Losing a daughter like Huong is more painful than losing an arm. Oh, Uncle! Please smother your pain when you hear the news.

Oh, poor Quang,[15] so many years you have waited faithfully for Huong to be yours. You will never have your dream now. Your Huong lies forever within the bosom of your homeland.

23 *April 1968*

A day of utter exhaustion: three seriously injured soldiers are brought in at the same time. All day I stand at the operating table, the tension in my head building toward the point of bursting. The men's wounds. Uncle Cong's heartrending cries when he hears his daughter Huong has died.

Duong is captured while on duty.[16] Can that joyful, eager boy endure the enemy's tortures? I feel so very sorry for him. My letter to Duong will never reach him; the messenger died and Duong is captured.

I hear a voice from far, far away singing a sad song: *Mother's heart is as vast as the ocean, her sweet lullabies as tender as a serene stream.* Was it Duong's voice the other night? Was it Duong crying out from his dark prison when he thought of his old mother, when he remembered her lifelong struggle to raise him, her sacrifices and joys invested in her beloved child?

---

[15]Quang was Huong's boyfriend.

[16]When Thuy refers to the enemy, she is referring to units of the Americal Division based in Quang Ngai. The 11th Light Infantry Brigade moved into Duc Pho in December 1967 and remained there for the period described in her diaries, occasionally reinforced by other units.

Many mothers will cry until their well of tears runs dry.

Oh, if I fall, my mom will be just like Duong's. She will suffer forever because her child has fallen in a fiery battlefield. Oh, Mom! What can I say when I love you a hundred, a thousand, a million times over and still I had to leave your side.

The enemy is still here; many mothers will still lose their children, and many husbands will lose their wives. The immensity, the enormity of our sufferings!

25 April 1968

There is more sad news: a group of Duc Pho cadres has been ambushed on its way back from a seminar in the province seat. I hear a few have sacrificed their lives to save their comrades. Nghia[17] is in the group. I wonder if anything has happened to my young brother. He is active, courageous, and capable of leading the group.

Oh, brother! What will I do if something happened to you? Will I cry through many quiet nights, will my tears run dry, or will a bright hostile flame flare within my heart against our enemy?

I have been waiting for your return, but now . . .

---

[17]Thuy considered Nguyen Tien Nghia her close friend, and refers to him as an "adopted brother."

26 April 1968

My heart is heavy as I read brother Tam's letter sent from H8[18]—
not a letter from M. The past is gone, why did you remind me of
it, Tam? You feel bad for me, but you unintentionally hurt me.
You tell me that M. is sick; you say you understand me, empathize
with me, but in fact you do not know me at all. Don't you understand that an educated woman has pride? If you did . . . it would
have been better if you had talked with me about important things,
my work, my awareness—and no more.

30 April 1968

Why are you still sad, Thuy? The critically wounded soldiers survive. Didn't the wan smiles on their pale faces bring you happiness? Didn't the recent praises for the clinic give you joy, Thuy?
And yet you are still sad.

This sorrow has seeped far into my heart like the relentless
monsoon rain willing itself deep into the earth. I have searched for
carefree joy, but I have failed, my mind already furrowed with
somber thoughts—there is no way to erase them. Perhaps I can
banish them by dedicating myself entirely to curing the wounded
and improving the clinic.

Oh, why was I born a dreamy girl, demanding so much of life?

By any measure, my life is a dream: I have a whole and good

---

[18]H8 is code for an organization under the NLF's administration in Duc Pho.

family.[19] I still have opportunities to advance my career, and I have tasks commensurate with my capabilities. People treat me with kindness. . . .

I demand too much of life, don't I?

Answer that, Thuy, Miss Stubborn, difficult to please.

1 May 1968

Once more, we celebrate Labor Day[20] in the jungle—it is a long, silent day, submerged in longings. I miss Hanoi, Dad, Mom, and my siblings terribly.[21] I doze off at noon and find myself coming back to see Mom and my sisters in the Supplementary School for Public Health Officers,[22] down that narrow road, to that gate at Mr. Nghiep's[23] house; I slip through the broken lattices of the gate as easily, as happily as I did in those younger carefree days.

---

[19]Thuy was counting her blessings, appreciating the fact that no one in her immediate family had been killed in the war. At the time, most Vietnamese families had suffered at least one casualty in the war.

[20]The Haymarket Riots of 1886 in Chicago, Illinois, are considered the origin of International Workers' Day (also known as Labor Day or May Day). In what is regarded as the first May Day parade, 80,000 Chicago workers—led by a labor leader and his wife and seven children—marched to demand an eight-hour workday and called for strikes to achieve that goal. The next day, two workers were killed in a strike, and during a peaceful rally on the following day to protest these deaths, a bomb was thrown into the crowd, killing police. Although no evidence linked them to the bombing, eight men were accused and found guilty. Three were hanged, sparking outrage and resulting in international protests. In commemoration of the Haymarket Riots, May 1 became a holiday to honor the working class in most socialist and communist countries.

[21]Thuy had four siblings including three sisters, Hien Tram, Phuong Tram, and Kim Tram; and a brother, Dang Hong Quang. Phuong is the oldest child after Thuy.

[22]Supplementary School for Public Health Officers was located on Giang Vo Street in the Ba Dinh District of Hanoi. After the war against the French, many staff members who managed the provincial and district-level public health departments needed more medical education because of their increased responsibilities. The Supplementary School for Health Officers was established to provide the requisite training. Thuy Tram's family lived from early 1957 to early 1967 in the resident housing attached to the school. Thuy's mother lectured there before becoming a lecturer at the College of Pharmacology in Hanoi.

[23]Dr. Tran Huu Nghiep was the principal of the Supplementary School for Public Health Officers from 1956 to 1965. He lived next door to Thuy's family.

I have been away from home over a year. Will this be my last year away? Suddenly, I remember the seasons before KN,[24] full of joy and hope . . . now(?) . . . Let's be like that time again, feel the joy of the victorious, hear the Revolution Song reverberating across the years: "On the road, on the road . . . defy sacrifices, seize power for the people."

4 May 1968

I let the conversation fade into silence. In the darkness, I sense their anxieties. They know that within this pregnant silence I'm trying to hold back the tears. My patients only want to talk to me. They care for me, but the more they say, the deeper I sink into misery. They ask me why I don't fight for my political rights, why am I worthy to be a Party member, yet I am not acceptable to the Party sub-branch?

Why, why, why? Who can answer that, my dear friends? Frankly, I cannot answer it. I can only offer you my silence to speak of that impasse.

It seems everyone is always saying: "Tram truly deserves to be a Communist Party member." And yet I am still not in that rank.

The more I wish to be accepted, the more miserable I feel.

These days I cannot escape this cloud of melancholy, but somehow I can still find the words, the acts, the ways to show affection. But every act of kindness, every shred of warmth is like a flame igniting the dry kindling in my heart.

---

[24]Vietnamese abbreviation for "The Uprising of the South" in 1960–61.

Everyone respects and loves me, but the Party remains so hard and ungenerous to me.

5 May 1968

Oh, M.! What can I say to you? I'm still madly, deeply in love with you, but my heart is scarred with anger and reproach. Did you say I don't understand you? No, I understand you, but not thoroughly enough. That's why I still grieve when everyone looks at me with pity. It hurts my pride. It is a deep wound impossible to heal, one I have resigned to bear all my life.

News that you have fallen gravely ill makes me very depressed. I feel your sufferings. If I were there by your side, I would take care of you the way a girl takes care of her lover—the way people want me to do. But the truth is not like that.

Oh, M.! You are not mine, but I still want my love to lessen your pain. What can I do now? Something tells me that I will not see you again, that this past farewell will be our very last. You looked at me as I walked away without glancing back, even though I could feel your eyes following me.

The seconds I spent in the arms of my beloved have become only images from the distant past.

6 May 1968

Every day I am plagued with things that give me headaches. I have already told myself I can't demand that all people be goodhearted; I have decided that "to live is to face the storms and not to cower before them." In fact, these trials of mine are merely end-of-summer storms, light and inconsequential.

Be happy with the affectionate smiles of the patients. Find cheer in the affection of your acquaintances, friends, and local comrades as well as of those who know you in the district and the province.

That is enough—oh, Thuy, don't ask for more.

As for the Party, it will have to see my worth. People who love and respect me outnumber those who hate me. In the final analysis, they only hate me because of their own jealousy.

9 May 1968

In life, one should be humble, but she should also have self-esteem and an independent spirit. If I am right, I should be proud of myself. A clear conscience is the most valuable medicine; I must understand it's the foundation of self-confidence. Why do I doubt myself when I know I did the right thing? You cannot live with sentiments alone—you must also possess a will. Do you understand that, you stubborn girl?

12 May 1968

Paris Negotiation Conference?[25] Will these be like the days of 1954? I follow the news with excitement, knowing that victories at the conference will be determined by victories at the battle-

---

[25]The Paris Peace Conference was convened in 1968 in Paris, France, with the goal of ending the war in Vietnam. The resulting Paris Peace Accords were signed in January 1973 by the governments of North Vietnam (DRV), the Provincial Revolutionary Government (PRG), the United States, and the Republic of Vietnam. The accords did not stop the fighting, which continued until April 30, 1975, when the PRG and DRV gained control of South Vietnam.

fronts. Let's prepare our spirit to enter the last stage of battle, to see who will survive. Whether I live or die, the days of boundless joy will come when true peace returns to our nation. This gracious land has endured more than twenty fiery years of war and misery; so much of our blood and tears have been shed. We do not regret anything exchanged for freedom and liberty.

14 May 1968

There is a line scribbled onto a tabletop: "Tram, My dear big sister . . ."

I recognized San's handwriting. This simple thing moves me. My affection for San grows day after day.

We once argued over the scenario that one of us must die for the other to live (he called me Big Sister even though I am younger than he). I wanted San to live because all his life he has known so little happiness, and because he is the only son of a widow who did not remarry after twenty-one years, just to raise him. Yet San insisted that I must live to go back to my mother, my younger siblings, and to the dear North that awaits me. It was so silly to discuss such nonsense, but in the talking, both "big sister" and "young brother" endeared themselves to each other.[26]

My feelings for San are sincere and purely innocent, and yet I'm worried some people might misconstrue our situation. San is three years older than I, married, and has a five-year-old child.

---

[26]San called Tram "big sister" as a sign of respect. Tram's reference to herself as his "big sister" and her addressing San as "younger brother" are indications that she accepted his respect and did not want to change the social hierarchy San proffered.

17 May 1968

The war goes on, death falls among us daily, like the flip of a hand. Just last night, Thin and Son were chatting with us. Thin asked Le to buy fabric for a shirt. Tonight they are two lifeless bodies within the earth of Duc Pho—this place where they had just set foot for the first time. Death takes us so easily; there is no way to prevent the losses. What sadness!

Lien is right: unless we live and love one another sincerely, someday we will regret when our friends die, and we will think we had not loved and cared for each other enough.

I have a physician's responsibilities and should maintain some degree of objectivity, but I cannot keep my professional compassion for my patients from becoming affection. I know that in their moments of illness, my patients come to love and depend on me. Even though we haven't met before, something ties them to me and makes them feel very close to me. They call me *chi hai,*[27] and refer to themselves as "younger brother" even though they are older than me. They tease and joke playfully to get my attention. In these perilous days, they give me joy and comfort. As for my personal matter, oh no, don't think of that, wipe away the clouds gathering on the horizon, don't let them bring a storm into your soul, Thuy.

---

[27]*Chi* means "older sister"; *hai* is the Vietnamese word for "two." In central and South Vietnam, to call someone "second sister" is to refer to her as the eldest sister. By calling Thuy *chi hai,* her patients are expressing their respect and affection.

20 May 1968

We say farewell to our patients today. They have recovered enough to return to their combat units. Instead of being joyful and happy, we are all sad, both physicians and patients. After over a month at the clinic, they have become like friends and family. It's wrenching to see them leave.

Today they are gone. Will they remember the long nights we talked, the nights we were on guard duty? Will they remember the day they assisted me with an injury while the whole staff of the clinic was away on rice transport duty?[28] They worked like professionals, laboring away all night by the oil lamp, meticulously cleaning the surgical instruments . . . those days were so fine! When are we going to meet again—and *will* we ever meet again, dear friends?

25 May 1968

These are dark days in my soul. Something presses heavily upon me. My wounded heart still bleeds from my own petty woes, but I also feel the weight of the inequities plaguing society. Ugly injustices happen all around me every day. There are worms and mites gnawing away within the Party; if those vermin are not eliminated, they will gradually erode the people's faith and love for the Party.

I am very disappointed the Party has not seen fit to let me join the ranks of its members so that I can fight these parasites. Perhaps that's why they still hesitate to accept me into the Party despite

---

[28]Each person was responsible for transporting his or her own supply of rice from the main storage depot, a two-day walk from the clinic.

urgent requests for an expeditious resolution of my political rights from all Party members in this sub-branch, from people in charge in the district and the province. The more I think about it, the sadder I feel. I want to confide my anger in dear ones, but I stay silent. Would anyone understand me?

Am I alone? Is there anyone else out there who suffers these repressive, frustrating days?

My life is filled with affection from all quarters, but I cannot find happiness because some people are jealous of the very love and affection I receive. Life always has a good side and a bad side, never the good side alone; so why you are still mired in misery as ever, Thuy?

29 May 1968

The days move slowly, heavily. Busywork helps me ignore the frustrations prickling me.

I ask you all, why? Why can't we use criticism and self-criticism to fight these frustrating problems? Why do we let old thoughts grow like tumors in our minds? Why is it that although we are right and in the majority, we cannot even win over a small minority? Why do we let the petty troublemakers cause difficulties for the community? Of course, there are good and bad people everywhere, and of course disagreement is natural in a society, but we must not surrender because of it. Our responsibility is to fight for what is right, to fight for righteousness. To win we must strive, think, and sacrifice our personal gains, perhaps even our own lives. That's it, Thuy! I will dedicate my lifelong career to securing the rights of the common man and the success of the Party! For better or for worse, I will hold the course with joy or sorrow—what else is there, Thuy?

31 May 1968

Today we had a major base evacuation[29] to evade the enemy's mopping-up operation.[30] The whole clinic was moved, an infinitely exhausting undertaking. It's heart-wrenching to see the wounded patients with beads of sweat running on their pale faces, struggling to walk step by step across narrow passes and up steep slopes. If someday we find ourselves living in the fragrant flowers of socialism, we should remember this scene forever, remember the sacrifice of the people who shed blood for the common cause. Who has brought this suffering upon us, comrades? They are the devils[31] robbing our country. . . . Oh, wounded warriors, I love you as my own brothers. Laugh even as you suffer, hold on to this immense optimism you have maintained for such a long time, regardless of countless difficulties.

1 June 1968

A brief dawn shower leaves the jungle green, the air pure, clean. A resplendent morning, yet my heart is full of longings, infinite

---

[29]The clinic's location was in Duc Pho District in Quang Ngai Province, in an area called the North Wing. Starting in April 1967, when she arrived in South Vietnam, Thuy was assigned there to help rebuild and manage a clinic that had been destroyed. On May 31, 1968, the clinic was forced to move, the first in a series of relocations.

[30]Thuy calls all American military actions "mopping-up" operations. The U.S. military used many terms. A "mopping up" action was to get rid of the enemy and its infrastructure following a search-and-destroy operation, an aggressive attack on an enemy stronghold.

[31]The U.S. military.

longings for the North. Longings for each line of trees on the streets, the *bang* and *sau*[32] with leaves shiny green after rain, the clean asphalt roads in the mornings. I remember the warm, simple room, the mornings reverberating with laughter, the radio chatting away in the middle of the room. I remember Mom, I remember Dad, I remember Phuong[33] and all my dear ones out there.[34] When will the sounds of guns stop for me to return to the beloved North? Will we still have those days together? War means losses. On this scorching soil of the South, it seemed one hundred percent of the families had suffered a loss. Death and suffering weigh heavily on each citizen's head. But the more they suffer, the more they loathe the enemy and the more fiercely they fight. Every southerner's life is a precious lesson for me. It's a privilege and honor to witness, isn't it?

Uncle Thao[35] said in a letter, "Don't be sad, Thuy. All of us out here look toward the dear South, each of our families has at least a dear one fighting there."

Many people are watchful of every step I make, waiting and believing that I will prevail in the end. In the last horrible dry season, I won, but I must still strive harder to win for the whole

---

[32]*Bang* is the malabar almond (*Terminalia catappa*); the fruit has a seed like an almond. The tree has a green canopy of thick leaves, each the size of a person's palm. *Sau* (*Dracontomelon duperreanum*) is another type of tropical tree.

[33]Born in 1947, Phuong is the next eldest sister.

[34]The Vietnamese thought of going from North Vietnam to central or South Vietnam as "coming in" or "entering," and going from central or South Vietnam to the North as "going out" or "exiting." This terminology came from the fact that North Vietnam was independent after 1954 above the 17th parallel. The South, on the other hand, was still under the control of the Republic of Vietnam and the U.S. military. The Vietnamese referred to traveling between the free and colonial regions as going "in" and "out."

[35]The youngest brother of Thuy's mother, Uncle Thao was eight months older than Thuy. Thao and Thuy played together as children and remained close as young adults. Although Thao dreamed of being a geologist, like all of Thuy's maternal uncles he enlisted in the North Vietnamese Army. Sent to Ukraine to learn to operate and drive tanks, he rose to the rank of major.

nation and . . . Oh, Thuy! Overcome these pains in your heart. Be joyful, let your camouflaging smile become a true smile of happiness. Don't let people whisper, "Why is Thuy sad?"

Why can I not hide the sadness behind this constant false smile?

2 June 1968

It rains this afternoon. The incessant downpour runs off the thatch roofs and the leaves, making a monotonous sound, strangely melancholic. For such a long time, I have forgotten the feelings of a Chu Van An[36] student chewing on the end of a pen, listening to the teacher's lecture, absentmindedly looking out through the drizzle to the blurred surface of West Lake, and thinking of silly matters. Why do those remote, bourgeois, adolescent sentiments return to me today—a cadre struggling in the perilous resistance? The past year has shown me a little more about reality. Life, real life, has two sides: (1) Love . . . life is full of love, sincere and generous people can still find love easily; (2) Selfishness . . . no matter how sincere and honest you are, you will suffer to know that there are selfish people who would not hesitate to use tricks and clever maneuvers to cheat and to rob you of every shred of credit, every minor privilege, sometimes for infinitely small things like a bite of food or some trivial object.

You want to live carefree, in total righteousness and love? No,

---

[36]Chu Van An School is one of the elite academic high schools in Hanoi, established by the French as the Lycée du Protectorate in 1906. After the August Revolution of 1945, the Vietnamese renamed the school in honor of a fourteenth-century scholar and educator, Chu Van An. It is on the shores of West Lake on the west side of Hanoi, the largest lake in the Red River Delta.

people will think that you are stupid and easy, that you let others climb onto your shoulders and straddle your neck and push your head down. Therefore you must fight, but to fight you must have experience and a solid foundation. The struggle is not between individuals or between groups, but between two schools of thought, the progressive and the old and obsolete. The conservatives are those who still hold on to the remains of bourgeois thought. The progressives are those who are fighting for the common endeavor. That is a normal rationale.

4 June 1968

The more I face reality, the more complexity I discover. Why do humans have so many demands? Never satisfied. The more one wants perfection, the more one has demands; and, down that path, one encounters ever more thorny obstacles—and yet if one does not persevere, one will surely fail.

Oh, this girl who lives with so many thoughts, don't think too much, it only brings you a heavy burden of pain and sadness. Let's find joys, let's live with forgiveness and sacrifices. Don't ask too much of life anymore.

Rain falls without respite. Rain deepens my sadness, its chill making me yearn for the warmth of a family reunion. If only I had wings to fly back to our beautiful house on Lo Duc Street,[37] to eat with Dad, Mom, and my siblings, one simple meal with watercress

---

[37]In 1967, after Thuy's departure for the South, her family moved from Giang Vo to Lo Duc Street in the Old Quarter of Hanoi. The location made it easier for Thuy's mother to visit whenever Thuy came back from the College of Pharmacology. The college had been evacuated from Hanoi to a remote mountain province near the Chinese border, owing to the American bombing. Thuy never lived in this house.

and one night's sleep under the old cotton blanket. Last night I dreamed that Peace was established, I came back and saw everybody. Oh, the dream of Peace and Independence has burned in the hearts of thirty million people for so long. For Peace and Independence, we have sacrificed everything. So many people have volunteered to sacrifice their whole lives for two words: Independence and Liberty. I, too, have sacrificed my life for that grandiose fulfillment.

15 June 1968

Oh, dear diary! Don't begrudge me these mournful lines. The victorious guns are sounding on all the battlefronts, North and South. Victory is nearing. . . . But in Duc Pho, sufferings are still heavy; day after day, blood pours, bones shatter. The saddest thing is that in those sufferings, I still cannot find equity and sincerity. There is no attempt to rid the Party of the pervasive pettiness and cowardice that are staining the honor of the title Party Member. Such attitudes erode the joy and eagerness of everyone working in the clinic. Oh, Thuy! Are you giving up when your folks, Party members, youths, and everyone else still support you? It is you who could not win over the few persons in the rank of cadre who serve only their own motives and pleasures. During the whole horrific dry season, I never felt pessimistic, I kept smiling despite the sufferings. Yet now I grieve. I am not afraid of the enemies on the battlefields, but I am afraid of the enemies, our very own, standing in the ranks of my comrades.

Maintain the fighting spirit, find the joy of the victors, and believe in yourself. I hope I will persevere to fight for my revolutionary career to the very end.

20 June 1968

A letter from Duong reached me; a letter wet with tears from the jail had slipped through legal hands. Duong wrote, "A simple handwritten letter, but please keep it as a memento because it holds my true heart. If I no longer exist, please remember that I worship and love you as always until death."

I had met Duong on a bright, sunny afternoon when, with a backpack on my shoulders, I was finding my way from the province to Duc Pho. The strange land of Pho Phong was welcoming me with open arms, especially Duong. I stayed at his family's home for only one day, but this little boy, Duong, clung to me. He was a student, intelligent and brave; in the socialist society he could have been a promising young writer. But in the enemy's school system, there were painful restrictions on a soul aspiring for knowledge, rich with dreams. I understood the feelings of such a student. In that briefest of time, we formed a bond, big sister and little brother. The next afternoon I returned to my post, while Duong stayed; afterwards he was captured while returning from duty. They had beaten him with incredible brutality, but he did not yield a single word about our organization. They were preparing to send him to Con Dao[38]; fortunately a former teacher begged for his stay. Now they sent him to their armed forces; he is in training. Will he escape to return to our revolutionary ranks when they put

---

[38]Con Dao (called Poulo Condor by the French) is an island off the southern coast of Vietnam where the South Vietnamese and U.S. military held prisoners in a former French prison. Some were kept in "tiger cages," which were underground spaces barely three feet high, the floors and walls of which were solid stone; iron bars formed the ceilings where the guards walked and through which they fed the prisoners. The inmates' leg muscles atrophied because the prisoners were unable to stand up, walk, or exercise.

him out onto the battlefield? Or will a bullet end his young, promising life?

28 June 1968

Oh, M.! Are you coming in again? Will you be the same M. as the one I knew from those Wednesday nights on that old road? You said you have never done anything wrong to me. If that's true, what will our lives be?

I am not a harsh or narrow-minded person, and yet I have arrived at the same conclusion as before. Behind this sad conclusion, there lies a whole history of thoughts. I don't know how to talk to you. No, M.! Please go, don't come to sow misery on my wounded heart again. It's impossible for us to be together, to be happy forever, even if we both survive this war.

30 June 1968

Autumn has not arrived, but the all the leaves in my world have turned brown. I have never felt this miserable and lonely. "To live is to face the storms and not to cower before them." Stand up, then, oh, Thuy! Even when the rain and gale are rising, even when tears have flowed in torrents, keep your spirit high, Thuy. Use your will, your faith in the just cause and the ideals of your life, to continue your journey on this dangerous path. Is there any victory without sweat and tears, thought and pain, blood and bones, Thuy?

You did not shed a tear for your broken love; then why do you feel so weak now, Thuy?

3 July 1968

July comes again to our jungle, with its southern wind bothering the trees, the early mornings cool, the moonlit nights serene. But in the blinding heat of the sun, this July is filled with suffering and anger. From the past years, I always remember the twentieth day of July, the day of the Geneva Accords.[39] I am fully aware of that day, of the great revolutionary history of this land, of the heroism of Vietnam; however, perhaps it was only six years ago.

It was a summer in Hanoi, July, when the night air enveloped us tenderly on that deserted road where I said farewell to my liberation soldier, sending him to the holy resistance. Since then, I have grown up every time July returns.

Now it's another July day—in the middle of a forested mountain, I am evading the enemy's mopping-up operation, caring for our injured soldiers. It is a strange, victorious pose. Only a Vietnamese can perceive victory in a retreat: the enemy hot on our heels, our shoulders aching beneath our heavy rucksacks, our blistered feet stamping a hasty retreat through the jungle and across the swift rivers.

---

[39]With the defeat of the French in May 1954, France and the Democratic Republic of Vietnam (DRV) signed the Agreement on Cessation of Hostilities in Vietnam (called the Geneva Accords) on July 20, 1954. The accords temporarily divided Vietnam into North Vietnam and South Vietnam at the 17th parallel until mandated elections could be held in 1956 to unify the country. Between 130,000 and 150,000 Viet Minh (Vietnamese who fought against the French), along with many of their family members, migrated north above the 17th parallel. Approximately 800,000 to one million Northern Vietnamese, mainly Catholics and French supporters, relocated to the South within the 300 days mandated in the accords. The promised elections were never held. A key provision of the accords was a guarantee against reprisals, but in 1959, President Ngo Dinh Diem launched a program to eliminate by killing, jailing, and intimidating southern families with family members who had gone to the North or were connected with the Viet Minh.

To Huu's[40] poem suddenly comes to mind:

Is there anywhere on this earth
Like the South agonizingly faithful
Like the South deftly courageous?

Our poet is certainly right. Is there anywhere else like this land? Is there anywhere else on earth where each citizen is a heroic fighter against the Americans? The land is soaked with the enemy's blood, and we have paid dearly for it. Each of our families carries a heavy mourning veil, and yet we still fight with unfaltering will and optimism.

Oh, Thuy, what an honor it is to stand in this rank of warriors!

5 July 1968

One of M.'s friends came to the clinic. He told me a story, hoping to rebuild my relationship with M., but I felt hurt and sad. The truth is M. doesn't deserve my heart anymore, so why does everyone urge me to forgive him? No, I will never accept a mended love, and he is not one to beg for forgiveness. M. insisted he had never wronged me, even in the slightest; that is not true. In fact, when we said farewell eight years ago, he admitted his

---

[40]Nguyen Kim Thanh (1920–2002), called To Huu, was Vietnam's most famous and influential revolutionary poet. Incarcerated by the French, Huu escaped in 1942 and joined the communist underground. To Huu moved quickly and successfully to assume various positions in the government, including the post of deputy prime minister. He was awarded the Ho Chi Minh Award, the highest award for literary and artistic accomplishments conferred by the Vietnamese state. His poetry is considered to be the best example of the revolutionary aesthetic, and is recited by schoolchildren throughout Vietnam.

mistake of giving his heart to a girl with whom he knew love and marriage should not be considered. It was the first in a string of mistakes.

Oh, M.! If you read these lines, what would you say? How many nights would you waste arguing your rationales?

6 July 1968

These simple letters cannot diminish my longing. Friends from everywhere send me their thoughts and affections, and yet I still feel lonely. I'm not a part of the Party's vanguard. My heart lacks the warming fire of the Party. I have come to the Party with a devoted and open heart, but it seems the Party has not treated me in kind. And M.—he does not deserve me, either. I have achieved none of the three pillars of life: Ideal, Career, and Love. That's why I cannot avoid being sad.

These days I miss home intensely. The forest wind reminds me of the sugarcane grove at the back of our house rustling noisily. In the blinding light of summer, I am transported back to the sunny corridors of Bach Mai Hospital,[41] where I had studied and played happily with friends. Every scene, every sound evokes memories of my days in the socialist North. How are things out there now?

---

[41]On December 22, 1972, American B-52 bombers hit Bach Mai Hospital in Hanoi, killing eighteen medical workers and patients. The nighttime bombings from December 18 to December 28 are often referred to as the "Christmas bombings," part of Operation Linebacker. In this largest air raid of the war, 15,000 tons of U.S. bombs were dropped near Hanoi and neighboring Haiphong Harbor. The bombing was a strategy by the United States to convince President Thieu of South Vietnam, who had balked at a draft agreement of the Paris Peace Accords, that the U.S. would aggressively defend South Vietnam. A month after the bombing, President Thieu signed the conditions of the Paris Peace Accords, the terms of which were nearly identical to the earlier draft.

Are Dad and Mom working in comfort?[42] Do they have any problems at their jobs? Oh, beloved Dad and Mom, your little girl is now fully immersed in the currents of life, a reality filled with love, hate, faith, pain, blood, tears, sweat, and victories earned with the sufferings of millions.

Do you believe that I will prevail? Your emotional, melancholic daughter, full of joy and determination, will prevail. That's a serious promise, Dad and Mom.

8 July 1968

The pictures and simple words from Mui[43] make me melancholy. "This time I do not write Thuy Tram a letter, not because I do not love my dearest friend. . . ." Why is that, Mui?

Bourgeois sentiments are always complex. It's strange that I still prefer to be like that than to be clear and simple like a farmer.

I am bourgeois only in sentiments, not in attitudes as some have claimed. How can they accuse me of having bourgeois attitudes when I can blend myself with all classes of citizens?

11 July 1968

It has been a long night talking with Luan—a student in the nursing class. Nights of conversation like these enrich and nurture me,

---

[42]Before the 1945 Revolution, Thuy's family was prosperous and considered bourgeois because of their financial status and level of education. During the war against the French, Thuy's parents lost everything and lived very simply in the countryside. Seven family members shared one room in a thatch-roofed cottage, but in that room were flowers, paintings, and, with Thuy's mother's encouragement, a rich spirit and, at their father's urging, music.

[43]Pham Mui is an artist who survived the war and lives in Da Lat.

expanding my understanding of the revolution and the communist's perspective of humanity.

Luan's life is more than theories; it is a real lesson. Since he was ten years old, Luan knew revolution, knew the hatred of a family isolated by the government, controlled by the Americans; he knew the affection for old mothers, young mothers, and innocent children, who suffer a thousand times under that regime. Night after night he crossed the fence of the strategic hamlet[44] to become a liaison and bring news to the cadres. At fifteen he took up arms to join the guerrillas. The hands of this twenty-one-year-old have killed the American robbers, and these are the same hands that have carried and held many of his comrades who fell defending our motherland. In the last dry season, Luan and his comrade guerrillas from Pho Vinh[45] resolutely dwelt in their suffocating tunnels all day, every day, and only emerged to act at nightfall. The weather and the hardships have left their marks on his young face, making him look older than his twenty-one years. In life, in experience, he is much older. I love and admire Luan. Despite a few weaknesses, he is one of the Vietnamese heroes.

---

[44] The concept of "strategic hamlets" was implemented during the American-backed regime of President Ngo Dinh Diem. These were centralized and fortified hamlets intended to isolate the population from "liberation" forces. The Strategic Hamlet Program was not successful and it fell apart after Diem's death. However, the U.S. military and ARVN forces continued to separate the villagers from the local resistance forces.

[45] The word *Pho* is used as a prefix for the names of most villages in Duc Pho. During the war against the Americans, the resistance divided Duc Pho into two geographical areas, the North Wing and the South Wing, with the town of Duc Pho as the center. The North Wing consisted of the villages Pho An, Pho Van, Pho Quang, Pho Phong, Pho Thuan, Pho Nhon, and Pho Ninh. The South Wing consisted of the villages Pho Hoa, Pho Vinh, Pho Khanh (Pho Hiep), Pho Cuong, and Pho Thanh. The smallest Vietnamese community unit was the hamlet. Several hamlets constituted a village, and many villages form a district. There are several districts in each province. Duc Pho is the district where Thuy was assigned to work as a physician in charge of a clinic that served both wounded military (PRG and NVA) and civilians. The village of Pho Vinh is in the district of Duc Pho in the province of Quang Ngai.

Late at night, the radio has long gone silent, but Big Sister and Young Brother are still awake, each with their own thoughts. I think of Peace, and I hope Luan and the thousands of young Vietnamese like him would survive this war. I hope they would have the opportunity to savor and enjoy the happy days to come. And, Luan, what do you think, Little Brother? Nourish your youthful hope and beliefs. I don't want to see suffering linger in eyes that still hold some shades of innocence.

14 July 1968

Thuan[46] crumples onto the bed and weeps uncontrollably at the news of his father's death. The sobs escape his attempts to restrain them. These cries of a young man full of fortitude and determination make me feel raw, as if someone has rubbed salt into my intestines. I feel the depth of his pain, but I do not know what I can say to comfort him.

Thuan lost his mother when he was a child. His father had struggled to raise three children.[47] Less than a month ago, Thuan's older sister was killed by an artillery round, leaving behind four innocent children. I could see the tragedies had left sad imprints in his young, beautiful eyes. Thuan has a younger sister. She left home at a young age to follow his footsteps in the revolution.

Since we first met, I've felt affectionate toward Thuan, not

---

[46]Thuan, also referred to as Brother Three, was the brother of Cho and Nhieu, to whom Thuy referred as her adopted younger brother.

[47]Thuy Tram made a mistake here; Thuan's father had four children, not three.

because he has the face of the student Arthur,[48] but because of his diligence in study and work, and the considerate way he treats others.

What can I say to comfort him now? His father died. Who will feed the three of them? To whom can they entrust the house and the farm? I cannot answer these questions myself.

Thuan sits in front of me, his eyes flustered. He is trying to force down the lump in his throat. His voice is shaky, broken: "Big Sister, permit me to return home for a few days to resolve family matters, then I will come back. I am the only one to resolve the disposition of my family's cattle and farm now. Please understand."

I don't know if he wants to say anything else, but he stops there.

I touch his hand lightly. It is hot with malarial fever. My voice is choked with emotions, too: "Young brother, go home and re-solve your family matters. Don't worry about the study; I and the class will take care of all that for you. I hope your resolve to stay the course with study and duty remains firm."

Go, young brother, go faithfully, bravely down this road of blood and fire that you have chosen.

18 July 1968

Received ten letters from the North at the same time. Each person has his own style, but they all care for me. It is as if each person has

---

[48]Arthur Montanelli, son of Cardinal Montanelli, is a revolutionary fighter in the novel *The Gad-fly,* by Ethel Lillian (née Boole) Voynich, published in 1897. (Voynich's father, George Boole, is famous for developing Boolean algebra, and her mother was a well-known feminist.) *The Gadfly* was considered a classic in Russia and China, and was mandatory reading in schools.

painted a portion of a larger picture, a lively portrait of the North. The dear North still stands firm despite the falling bombs and bullets. The war has not hindered our nation on the road to victory (of course it has suffered grievous wounds, but it marches forward like a wounded soldier who still has a smile on his lips and determination and conviction in his heart). I've met so many brave young men in this heroic South. Today, through these letters, I have visions of such a man, infinitely glorious.

20 July 1968

The days are hectic with so much work piling up, critical injuries, lack of staff personnel; everybody in the clinic works very hard. My responsibilities are heavier than ever; each day I work from dawn till late at night. The volume of work is huge, but there are not enough people. I alone am responsible for managing the clinic, treating the injured, teaching the class.[49] More than ever, I feel I am giving all my strength and skills to the revolution. The wounded soldier whose eyes I thought could not be saved is now recovering. The soldier whose arm was severely inflamed has healed. Many broken arms have also healed. . . . All these successes are due mainly to the nurses and me working day and night at the patients' bedside.

To the students, I offer my knowledge of medicine. I teach the class not only because it is my duty, but also because of my sisterly affection for my students, who are like my own younger siblings.

---

[49]In addition to providing medical treatment, Thuy taught young medical workers, mainly in basic nursing skills.

The nation's traitors have denied them the opportunity to learn. I want to give them a full education, to teach them everything I know. How I love the Thuans, the Liens, the Luans, Xuans, Nghias, each with his or her own situation, but they are very much alike: diligent, striving to achieve the pinnacle of knowledge. Thuan has just cried for his father's death; the two deaths in his family are still heavy on his chest, but he could still muster a smile to his pale lips for his comrades. Thuan could still sing, laugh, and participate in class discussion passionately. Looking at Thuan, I love and admire him so much.

Lien studies and works at the clinic. She rises at dawn to work, and labors till dusk like a bird, quickly and diligently. She joyfully takes the lead in every struggle—hers is also an example from which I need to learn.

How can I count all these unnamed heroes who rise up in this burning land of the South?

25 July 1968

I came to sit by Lam's bedside today. A mortar had severed the nerves in his spine, the shrapnel killing half of his body. Lam was totally paralyzed. His body was ulcerated from the chest down. He was in excruciating pain.

Lam is twenty-four this year, an excellent nurse from Pho Van. Less than a month ago, he was assigned as supplement to the District Civil Medical Department. The enemy came upon Lam while he was on the road during his recent assignment; Lam tried to get into a secret shelter, but the Americans were already upon him when he opened the cover; the small shrapnel painfully destroyed his life. Lam lay there waiting for death. In the North, a severed spinal cord is already a hopeless case, let alone here. Lam knows the severity of his injury and is deep in misery and depression.

This afternoon as I was sitting next to him, Lam handed me a letter from Hanh (Lam's young wife), then said in a low voice, "Big Sister, you and the other sisters here—you are my family— you have dedicated yourselves to nurturing me. What for? I will die sooner or later; if I live, I will only bring more hardships for you and the family." A single tear rolled down Lam's gaunt cheek.

My heart was breaking for him, but I didn't know what to say. If I were Lam, I certainly would have said the same. But I couldn't stop encouraging him. . . . Oh! War! How I hate it, and I hate the belligerent American devils. Why do they enjoy massacring kind, simple folks like us? Why do they heartlessly kill life-loving young men like Lam, like Ly, like Hung and the thousand others, who are only defending their motherland with so many dreams?

28 July 1968

Brother Kha[50] was captured!

A tragedy. Just the other day Kha held my hand—a warm, intimate touch shared by siblings and colleagues from the same hometown. Big Brother, it was only a few days ago that you worked next to me, your little sister, both of us bent over the operating table. Your handwriting is still imprinted clearly on the patient record. Where are you today, in chains or in a torture chamber?

---

[50]A close physician colleague of Thuy Tram's father and a friend of the Tram family, Kha was captured and sent to Con Dao prison. After his release, Kha accepted a position as an army doctor in Can Tho, near Ho Chi Minh City.

On his departure that morning (20 July), Kha certainly never thought of falling into the enemy's hands, so he cheerfully said good-bye to everyone. He held my hand and said in a low voice, "I'm leaving, Thuy," then he took a few steps and spoke louder. "I'll return in about ten days, fifteen at most."

Dear Kha, now I feel more affection for you than ever. This simple, sincere bond has been with me since I first wore the red scarf on my shoulder, since the day when I used to call you "Uncle Kha."[51] Remembering you, I remember the whole chain of peaceful days. There was a beautiful house, little Kim's large brown eyes. . . . Will I ever see you again? Your rucksack is still here; I feel a stab of pain in my heart whenever I see it.

4 *August 1968*

The days are still filled with ever more duties. Difficulties and challenges spring up every hour, every minute, and yet I feel warm with confidence. Is it the smile of that young student that has calmed my inner turmoil, the smile on lips shadowed by the sadness of two recent deaths in his family? Is it the lasting echo of his off-note singing despite his sorrows? I am reminded again to strive toward this wondrous optimism. Yes, I will learn and hold firm the revolutionist's belief that you, my comrade, taught me through your strong heart and perseverance.

---

[51]A Vietnamese child traditionally calls his or her parent's colleague "uncle" or "aunt." Once the child becomes an adult and the age difference is not so pronounced, the younger person may address the older person as "big brother" or "big sister." This is usually done at the behest of the older person. By saying she "wore the red scarf," Tram is referring to her teenage years, when she was in the Ho Chi Minh Pioneer Children's Union. The red scarf was part of the uniform of Ho Chi Minh's front-guard youth.

And I am delighted to hear the song ringing again after many tiresome hours of work.

I feel so happy to find many eyes turning to me with understandings, affections, and respects. The eyes of students waiting for me to come to the class, the eyes of patients looking for me in the patients' ward. . . . That's enough, Thuy. Don't ask for more. The whole of Duc Pho has reserved its tender affection for you. That's the greatest privilege.

Sister Hai has brought sad news: Brother Dung died, captured and killed on site.

What agony!

Must I keep filling my small diary with pages of blood? But, Thuy! Let's record, record completely all the blood and bones, sweat and tears that our compatriots have shed for the last twenty years. And in the last days of this fatal struggle, each sacrifice is even more worthy of accounting, of remembering. Why? Because we have fought and sacrificed for many years; hope has shone like a bright light burning at the end of the road; today, when we are close to our goal, so many of us have fallen. . . .

8 August 1968

Autumn has not arrived, but the mornings are already cold. Is it the chill in the mountain forest that has made me lonely? No, Thuy, don't lie to yourself. You are sad—it is a sadness that cannot be denied, regardless of how much affection others shower upon you. Oh, Thuy! How can I deal with life when there are such small-hearted people and cowards in our midst? What can you say? A clear stream, though it has stagnant pools and hidden rocks, is still beautiful. We appreciate the whole stream in its poetic entirety without begrudging its small stagnant parts.

Oh, M.! Are you like a beautiful, flowing stream marred by shoreline stagnations?

I am a hiker in the middle of the forest. What do I think? "I hope that was only a curse in a fairy tale. Those things should not be in your soul."

Did you tell me to forget the things that affected our trust in each other? No, M.! The trust stemming from ten years of waiting and longing does not erode easily, but when it cracks, it's hard to repair.

So I don't know what to say. Oh, M.! What will happen if you don't return from this journey? Oh, why do we only bring each other pain? Why do you keep sowing pain in my earnest heart?

14 August 1968

We've had afternoons like this, golden light glowing softly through the door. Beyond the forest is silence. . . . Has the distance spared us the searing heat of battle? Quietly I listen to the murmuring discussions of students studying for the exam. Students! How I adore them, my younger sisters and brothers, especially Thuan, a cadre of the class. He is diligent, hardworking, innocent, and considerate. I love him for his extraordinary will and his tragedy—the two deaths in his family still weigh heavily on his chest. From time to time I find him sitting alone, deep in thought, sighing privately, but in front of others, he always maintains his eagerness and enthusiasm.

Seeing the way Thuan studies and works, few people could comprehend the magnitude of his tragedy.

Thuan is like my adopted young brother Nghia, full of spirit and character. I have an urge to consider Thuan as a young brother and to treat him accordingly to bring him some cheer. Should I? I must think carefully!

Goodbye, Khiem.[52]
My dear friend who fell in the heroic land.
Oh, Khiem! I swear to avenge you until my dying breath.

16 AUGUST 1968

When I left Pho Hiep[53] on the afternoon of the twenty-sixth of October '67, the front yard of Thuong's house was full of people coming to say farewell. Emotions made me awkward. I didn't know what to do. I sat down beside Thuong's mother to gather yams into a basket. When I looked up, I was surprised by a pair of eyes staring at me. They were very kind black eyes brimming with tears. They were immensely sad and filled with affection. Those were Khiem's eyes.

I knew Khiem from the horrific days of the dry season of 1967, when I came to serve at Pho Khanh. That young teacher came to me with an open heart full of sincerity and respect. I saw his goodness immediately. People who went through a student life can understand each other easily. During the days in the secret

---

[52]Vo Khiem, a teacher and dear friend of Thuy's, was killed on August 8, 1968. Thuy continues to mention him in the diary through March 1969, reflecting on his death.

[53]Pho Hiep is in the area referred to as the South Wing by the PRG. Thuy had a special affection for the people of Pho Hiep, and when she departed, she wrote a poem in their honor.

underground chambers, I told Khiem about Pavel[54] and *The Gad-fly,* about my favorite poems.

> *Who wrote your name on the list of heroines?*
> *By the rows of white tombstones in the middle of the field*
> *Missing you, I called: you, comrade.*
> *One heart among a thousand hearts.*[55]

Khiem loved the poems "Nui Doi" and "Que Huong," too.[56] Khiem told me about his life in and out of jail. He was incarcerated in jails all over the province as well as in Hue. . . . The countless beatings by the enemy made him weak and thin.

At the beginning it was only the warmth of camaraderie, but later it became a pure and sincere friendship. After serving in the lowlands for a term, I returned to the base. It's nearly one year since we were together, but I still feel his sad eyes, rimmed with tears, looking at me as we parted.

No one could have guessed that that good-bye would be our final farewell. Khiem died! In a mopping-up operation, the Americans found his secret chamber; Khiem jumped out and hurled his only grenade at the enemy. Scared, the bloodthirsty devils threw themselves down to the ground. Khiem ran a short way, but the cursed grenade did not explode. The bandits jumped up, chased

---

[54]Pavel Korchagin is a character in *How the Steel Was Tempered. Ruoi Trau* is the Vietnamese name for the novel *The Gadfly* (see note 48).

[55]Excerpt from the poem "Nui Doi," ("The Twin Hills") by Vu Cao.

[56]"Nui Doi," by Vu Cao, and "Que Huong" ("Homeland") by Giang Nam, were beloved by Vietnamese adolescents during the resistance against the French.

Khiem, and shot him. Khiem died, his once-kind eyes now wide open, full of hatred, his youthful, lustrous hair now drenched with blood and dust, the sand of the nation bound to the hair of the young hero. His shirt was tattered and bloodstained. This was the shirt he wore when I first met him, the same shirt he'd worn when we worked our way through a narrow, treacherous trail full of tiger-tongue thorns[57] on the 31, 32, 33, Quy Thien, on the 15, 19 "Uncle Trung Hai."[58]

And it was with this very shirt that he came back from Pho Khanh one beautiful moonlit night. A cold wind blew in from the sea and made him shiver. I gave him one of Que's shirts. It was a simple red shirt that matched the warmth of his words that day: "Oh, Thuy, in this life, besides my father and mother, I do not love anyone more than you."

Khiem sacrificed himself! I was stunned at the news, I could not believe it was the truth. When I was certain Khiem had died, I did not cry. I was calm. I used my will to conquer my emotions. But as each minute passed, the pain grew and then tears flooded my eyes. I cried alone by the late-night lamp, salty tears rolling down my face and soaking my shirt. Oh, Khiem! Is there any way you can hear me one more time? Hear my promise to avenge you, a promise full of rage, wrought in excruciating pain and blinding hatred, a promise with the longing for you that will never fade. Do you hear me, Khiem, immortal friend of my heart?

---

[57]The tiger-tongue vine has hard, sharp thorns.

[58]Code names for hamlets in the village of Pho Hiep.

Good-bye Khiem,
My dear friend who fell in the heroic land.
Oh, Khiem! I swear to avenge you until my dying breath.

16 AUGUST 1968

Parted with Khiem that day, wishing for a reunion,
Now . . . "who knew the day we parted was the last
   good-bye."

16 AUGUST 1968

20 *August 1968*

With so much frustration and little joy or hope, I pen my application for Party membership. Why do they fill the path of a bourgeois with spikes and thorns?

Of course, social class is the obvious issue, but beyond that I see one thing clearly. Some people in charge have managed to create an impasse against my admission with petty criticisms.

What is there to say, that's life!

No matter how much effort you have shown through your achievements, as a bourgeois, you are still below a person of the labor class who has only just begun to comprehend Party ideals.

When Huong was alive, she used to encourage me that it was an advantage to be a bourgeois! What advantage? The advantage of facing even more difficulties and hardships, Huong? I'm like a child who has missed her mother for a long time, and returns home to find an indifferent and coldhearted stepmother who is busy pampering her own children. Millions of people have created a great mother—the Party—but in those millions there are certainly more than one who behave very poorly, much like Cinderella's stepmother.

27 August 1968

A critical operation is successful, a ruptured kidney mended.

The bleeding has stopped; the patient's urine has become clear and normal. A life saved should be a great joy, but somehow I feel apathetic and inadequate before my smiling patient, unmoved by his respectful eyes. Is it because I know I have stemmed but one bloodflow while countless others are still bleeding? I must mend all the wounds of our nation. The Americans are upon us like bloodthirsty devils, stealthily sinking their fangs into our bodies. Only when we have chased them all out of Vietnam will our blood stop pouring into the earth.

28 August 1968

I received Thuy Phuong's letter from Qui Nhon. I have never met this beautiful niece, but I love Phuong for her enthusiasm and her heroic life.[59] At the beginning of spring, Phuong was injured and captured in an American ambush while on her way to join the armed forces. She escaped the jail recently, but she is still weak and cannot return home.

---

[59]Phuong and Tram were not actually niece and aunt, but the two women referred to themselves by this relationship to indicate their affection for one another.

Phuong's letter, the soft handwriting on a long sheet of type-writer paper, suddenly reminded me of Khiem, and I felt for Khiem immensely. Khiem's classmate, Phuong was very fond of Khiem. If Khiem were still alive, I would have hoped that something beautiful would develop between them. Today Phuong returned from jail, but Khiem was gone. Oh, Phuong, you're right: happy are people who fall in glory like Khiem. As for us, we must live with the fire of hatred burning brightly in our hearts, we must burn the enemy with it. Today, remember, Phuong, remember that the land has been soaked with blood and tears for twenty-three years.

30 August 1968

Each day the news of victories in both parts of the country over-whelms me with joy, but it also fills my heart with immense sadness.

Why? Because as long as American bandits exist in our land, there are sufferings and losses; there can be no happiness.

Brother Lien came to visit; he asked me why I have been treating M. that way. Oh, why, my brother, there are thousands of reasons! I don't know any other way to resolve my relationship with M. Do you think I am not suffering? The smile on my lips is not the smile in my heart. I don't want to dwell on these matters. The more I think about them, the more I feel immensely sad. I don't know whom to trust. Trust M. or trust the thousands of rumors? Whom should I follow? Follow my dream or follow a reality that many people have shown me?

Don't ask any more, the sounds of guns are reverberating on the battlefields, listen to them and rally to the call, "All for the front, all for victory."

1 *September* 1968

I feel very sad sending my friend a gift. I don't want to give him just an object, he certainly doesn't want that either. Then why did I send the gift without including a note, an explanation, or intimate words?

Who can see my heart? I am a girl full of love and generosity, but I'm also uncompromising and proud.

A small incident happened today. What does it tell me? Is that a lesson? No, no lesson can be so bitter and insensible. It is only jealousy, a seemingly essential trait of human nature. If I deem it essential, then why do I still feel bitterly sad? This is an organization, a milieu where difficulties and sufferings test a bourgeois girl each hour, each minute. It's nothing. I have lived in comfort, now I should taste the pain and bitterness of life. How should I live? It is better to raise my head and live with a bright, lucid perspective, with high and beautiful ideals. "Uphold firmly the spirit of a communist, the soul as pure as crystal, as hard as diamond and brilliant with the aura of faith. . . ."

Even so, I still have feelings of profound grief, bitterness, and loneliness. M. left, Khiem sacrificed his life, Van departed, Second

Sister[60] departed, Nghia and Thuong departed. . . . It is not easy to confide matters of the heart to anyone around me.

5 September 1968

It is a night of farewells for the students. My heart feels restless. On the familiar bench, big sister and young brother sit side by side; I listen to your loving words, young brother, but you're leaving to-morrow. You go back to the fighting, to countless difficulties and perils. I hope you'll persevere. I understand you, the young brother full of determination, full of faith and strength. But . . . what can guarantee that you will live till the day of victory! You are ex-tremely courageous—I am proud of you, but in the depths of my heart I still worry . . . the worry is very reasonable, but somehow also very wrong. The worry of seeing a dear one throwing himself into a life-and-death duel.

I look into your shining eyes beneath those long lashes, and I read in there all the things you want to say: your love and concern for me and the longing when we are apart. I understand, I promise you I will deserve your faith.

6 September 1969

This afternoon the forest, usually boisterous with human voices, suddenly grows quiet, leaving only the cicadas' laments and the howl of the wind in the treetops. A chill in the air, is it the storm

---

[60]Tran Thi Khiem was a close friend of Thuy, whom Thuy referred to as "Second Sister."

or autumn? I suddenly feel cold, a cold that numbs both flesh and soul. Longings engulf my soul. Is this the same autumn afternoon when the evening fog stretched vaguely over the fields outside Hanoi, when I alone rode my bicycle home from the campus on that empty road? The cold wind whistling through the roadside trees, I remembered shivering slightly as I passed a tree whose trunk was forked cleanly into two branches.

This afternoon the wind is cold, and so is my heart. I miss not one person but many: Dad, Mom, siblings, uncles in the North, the young brothers down in the plains, struggling day and night in the fatal duel, the dear comrades who fell for tomorrow's victory. And who else? The young brothers and sisters, the young colleagues who once clung to me and studied diligently with me. All of you have given me tremendous love for . . . Far from you I am struck with an immense longing.

To Huu says,

> *What yearning is like the yearning for a lover*
> *When the moon rises on the mountaintop or the afternoon*
>   *light shines on the field?*

Somehow it seems to me my poet fails to express it correctly this time. My longing for M. is so blurry I have even forced myself to forget it. Or maybe To Huu is right. . . . M. is not my lover! M. has not treated me like a lover. He is only a friend. And as a friend, that's how it is! It isn't easy for me to say something like this today, is it, M.?

8 September 1968

The seventh storm! There are many storms in the North this year, all major ones. Here, within the depth of the forest, it is silent, but out there the wind howls. Many houses will collapse, many trees will fall. Are there casualties, my beloved North?

As with the weather in the North, another storm rages within my heart. Worries and longings. Oh, the North, stay firm, be triumphant as in the victorious days. Certainly, there are many obstacles. Young men have already left for the battlefront, and the womenfolk at home surely have a hard time withstanding the storm.

This evening I feel as though I were in a small house in a hamlet by the sea. The wind is rather chilly. Holding a sweater in my hands, I feel my heart growing restless with yearnings. The cold wind of autumn has arrived; this is my second autumn away from home, the second autumn since I hurled myself into the war.

And where are you this afternoon, my dear ones? Dear brothers and sisters down in the plains, a friend rushing into the line of fire, a dear one resting within the bosom of our motherland. Oh, Khiem, the evening has turned a faint shade of violet. There, you might hear the murmurs of lapping waves. There, you might see the familiar road from Qui Thien[61] to New Hamlet. Do you remember those violet evenings? Why are you silent? You are already silent; you cannot answer me ever again.

---

[61]Qui Thien is a hamlet in Pho Hiep village.

10 September 1968

Reading Thuan's letter, I am moved by his earnest and sincere longing. Suddenly, a warmth blossoms in my heart as though a small fire has been lit. Oh, Thuan, your words are one of the sources of encouragement for me, urging me to persevere and complete my duties. Your will and your struggle will always be examples for me.

So, you're sad, and you ask me why I don't accept you as my young brother the way I have accepted Thuong[62] and Nghia? It's because I want a holy and noble relationship between brother and sister. I have feelings for you but I certainly do not understand you completely, and likewise you certainly haven't understood all about me. Therefore, let's wait, brother.

I sit long into the night beside the lamp, thinking much about you, an intelligent brother, full of strong will. Let's respect the beautiful and lofty feelings we have for each other. Let's be faithful to our feelings and be worthy of our trust in each other.

15 September 1968

Attending the districtwide women's conference, I feel happy to live within the warmth and love of my elder comrades. Life doesn't consist of only moments of loneliness.

---

[62]Tran van Thuong, Thuy's close friend whom she called young brother, was captured on April 27, 1970. He was sent to Con Dao prison and was released to North Vietnam in 1973 under the terms of the Paris Peace Accords. These conditions required that he stay in North Vietnam. In 1975, after the war ended, he returned to Duc Pho.

On the way back, walking along a small stream, I miss Thuan deeply. This is only a feeling of a sister for a brother, and yet it makes me strangely restive. I imagine Thuan returning from duty to a cold house, a dim light on the altar; he eats dinner alone and then hangs a hammock to rest, a cigarette in his lips, tendrils of smoke roaming the empty house. No one else is left except friends and comrades. At home, Thuan is alone. I want my sincere feelings to warm his unfortunate life. I have sent him a letter, but I don't think I have expressed much of my thoughts. Oh, Thuan! Do you deserve my affection?

17 September 1968

Sister Cap[63] recounts the day of Khiem's sacrifice. The story breaks my heart. Khiem is dead, his head crushed, his arm and leg on one side of his body blown off. Khiem lay on the sand of his homeland. When Khiem's father, who was injured with his arms bound, blood gushing out of his shoulder, saw his son's body, he could not stem the tears flooding from his eyes. There was great fatherly love in those eyes burning with pain and hatred.

Khiem died. His mother stood before her son's body, but could not utter a word. She still has not recovered, her waking hours filled with tears for her son.

Oh, Khiem! From the world beyond, can you see the pain of the living? The tears of your parents have not dried, and the heart of this friend of yours is still bleeding.

---

[63]Sister Cap was a nurse in Thuy's clinic.

19 September 1968

At the districtwide youth conference, I am living among the joys of adolescents who have grown up in the struggle. I meet the teenagers and listen to some of their reports.

Hoang, fourteen years old, has killed five American soldiers in the first six months, turned over two tanks with his own improvised weapons, and captured seven enemy guns including two mortars and other types.

An Pho Chau has captured five guns, two of which were mortars, and one radio.

The little brothers are already heroes at such an early age.

Be proud of our youths!

27 September 1968

I've been admitted into the Party.

My clearest feeling today is that I must struggle to deserve the title of "communist." As for the joy, why is it so small compared with the significance of the joyful day? Why was that, Thuy? Probably it is like what I said the other day: for a child exhausted by hunger for her mother's milk, the milk no longer tastes so sweet.

During meditation to remember those who have sacrificed for the Party's mission, I truly miss the dear ones in Duc Pho who have fallen in this life and death struggle.

5 October 1968

I lost an amputation patient. He was sixty years old but still strong, a veteran Party member who had been in the fight for twenty-three years. His family and the clinic staff tried their best, but we couldn't save the old man.

The community and his son accept that I did everything I could, but I am still painfully disappointed. Why did he die? Was it my technique? It wasn't that. Although it was my first amputation, I stayed calm and adhered to the surgical protocols. Then why? Was it the unsuccessful plasma transfusion? I don't know what to say: we got the vein, then missed it again and again because of the old man's continuous thrashing. What a tragedy!

Why can't I draw any lesson from this untimely death?

6 October 1968

There is jealous gossip about me. Some people are envious of the affection others have for me. I think about these gossips some-times. In the end, I don't think everyone loves me because I'm a physician. The warm letters and gifts show affection for a dear friend, not tribute to a doctor. These are merely tokens of fondness from a sister, a young brother, a big brother, and a friend. But, at times, I wonder about the sincerity of those sentiments. Why are there so many little brothers, so many friends giving me such a unique position in their hearts?

8 October 1968

The bright light of early autumn floods the forest and carries a wind that withers both lips and hearts. Yearning once more . . . a yearning as deep as the ocean embracing Vietnam. I miss my secret, kind friend who lives in a small house at the end of Doi Can Street,[64] the playful young sister who pins her long, soft hair so high, the young brother of the South who sent me a farewell letter before going away to school, the dear young brother who has glittering eyes beneath such long lashes. And I really miss my dear friend who has been laid to rest forever on the coast of our motherland.

Oh, my country! When will these yearnings diminish, when will our country know peace? I know the victorious day is near, but somehow I feel my happiness is very far away. Can I possibly see that day of happiness again? "A communist loves life dearly, but can take death just as lightly if necessary." Be willing to die, but also be willing to love life dearly, this precious thing that our people have paid for with blood and tears for twenty-three years.

10 October 1968

Commemorated the liberation of the capital of the inflamed South.[65] A consummate passion engulfs my soul.

---

[64]Doi Can Street is in Hanoi.

[65]The Vietnamese defeated the French at Dien Bien Phu in 1954. What was remarkable about the event was that a small grassroots national effort grew into a major, organized military force, able to defeat a major European power. Vietnamese General Vo Nguyen Giap called his strategy "nibbling and full-scale attack." The Vietnamese dug trenches in the hills encircling the French. Then, from the outer trenches, tunnels were dug closer to the French. Gathering 70,000 Viet Minh troops from all over Vietnam, the Vietnamese hauled and dragged heavy artillery guns to

Hanoi was liberated . . . the tattered images of the last French soldiers withdrawing from Hanoi to the north side over Long Bien Bridge.[66] Hanoi was liberated fourteen years ago. Through storms of bombs and bullets, our Hanoi still stands strong. I still hear the pure and clear laughter of students in the courtyard of the Mam Non School on Hang Bong Nhuom Street.[67] I still hear the clanking of the electric tram in the streets. Oh, Hanoi, as much as I miss it, I feel for Saigon, Hue, and the hundreds of cities that still suffer the flames of battle. This war is an unprecedented atrocity, and we have fought back with unparalleled courage and perseverance. Who will survive, who will have been lost when our nation gains its independence? If I die, I have already savored the days of socialism. There are still hundred of thousands of people growing up who only knew sufferings and hardships, like Khiem, Huong, Ly, Tuan, Hung Tho . . . and there are many more who have fallen without knowing a single day of happiness. How painful!

11 October 1968

A friend reveals the yearning in his heart to me, and then he asks me for an answer. I reply without hesitation that I only consider

---

the tops of hills, from which positions they could fire down on French troops and into the sky at paratroopers attemping to resupply them. The French were closed off from the outside world, under constant fire, and taking casualties. They appealed to the Americans, and some American advisers suggested the use of a nuclear bomb. President Eisenhower would not enter into conflict without the British, and Winston Chruchill refused, hoping that the Geneva Peace Talks would resolve the situation.

[66]Built by the same construction firm that erected the Eiffel Tower and the Statue of Liberty, the Long Bien Bridge in Hanoi was completed in 1902 and spans the Red River. It was a vital link for North Vietnam, since all supplies transported by train from China via the port of Haiphong crossed it. The bridge was frequently bombed by the U.S. military.

[67]Mam Non is the name of the kindergarten school. It means "young shoots" or "young buds." It was located on Hang Bom Nhuom Street in central Hanoi.

him a friend, nothing more. Then I say, "My heart has stowed away all my private dreams to focus on my duties."

My reply is true to my conscience, but not to my heart. My love for M. still makes my heart bleed. I want to forget. Pride has helped me forget M., but there are moments when I grieve like someone who has lost a valuable object and cannot find it again. Tonight I reopen the old letters, and at once my heart aches and fills with anguish. Oh, M.! Your words have not washed from the pages, but somehow you have already faded from my life. You have buried a beautiful love; you have taken lightly the very thing you have respectfully held for the last eight years. Everybody tells me things will pass, and we will reunite as all have hoped. But in my heart, I know it's over—how can a broken mirror be whole again? How can a spilled cup be full again?

12 *October 1968*

Reading Phuc's letter, I am very angry with him. He speaks outrageously without facts. For me, it's a lesson about the way people express their opinions.

I meet with a number of people at the big gathering for guerrilla warfare. I suddenly feel so close to all the heroes of Duc Pho who have gathered here in victory. I am glad to be considered an acquaintance of many folks from Pho Phong to Pho Thanh. The whole population of Duc Pho has received me with open arms. . . . Discreetly, a young brother has slipped a letter full of affection into my hand. What can I do to deserve the love of the people of Duc Pho?

13 October 1968

I see Thuan again after a little more than a month. A little more than a month, but it seems so long. I am so glad he is still strong and has matured in his duties.

Living close to him, I treasure the moments we share. The war continues. How can we tell who will survive and who will die, my young brother? I have the feeling Thuan hasn't told me certain things about himself. Why is that? You don't really trust your big sister? It's unreasonable to be hesitant. Didn't you tell me that you loved me with complete sincerity? Then answer me, my young brother.

20 October 1968

I say farewell to Thuan. Both of us find it hard to talk about our feelings. Young brother, I will anxiously follow your every step, for the enemy's guns still reverberate in Pho Cuong.[68] You are going where a thousand dangers await. How can I be calm?

Staying behind, I understand your silence. You stand there holding an umbrella, looking at me but not knowing what to say. A good-bye is meaningless because it cannot express your feelings for me. I suddenly remember you saying that, like Khiem, you love me more than anyone else in this life, that now you focus your life only on your assignments and on your love for me. Listening to you then, I was extremely moved. I believed you, but still asked

---

[68]Pho Cuong is a mountain village in Duc Pho District. Xuan Thanh is a hamlet in Pho Cuong village.

myself: Can this be true? Why do I deserve your great love? Could this be the noble reward for a revolutionary?

Now I understand why people can sacrifice their whole lives for our cause, and how they can remain absolutely faithful to the revolution. The revolution has forged a noble people and bound them into a unit firmer and more solid than anything in this life. Could anything make one prouder than to be part of this family of revolutionaries?

23 October 1968

It's turning cold after the rainy days.

Today, in the cold of early winter, somehow I feel the hours and minutes of reunion I have with my dear ones are more precious than ever.

The war grows fiercer each day. When can that dream of peace be realized in both parts of the country, dear ones? It's not despair, it's only the sensible dream of mine and of thirty million Vietnamese. The long-held dream of many years is ripe!

In the long, cold, windy nights, the thin blanket is not warm enough. I wake up and become restless with longings. A thousand images of dear ones appear in front of my eyes. But his face, with his telling eyes beneath those dark curls, is absent. I no longer see him in my dreams. Should I blame myself for this? No! I am not a heartless person. Friendship and kinship are enough to move me deeply. But . . . the curly hairs have fallen over his face, covering all that I treasure. His eloquent eyes have quieted long ago. How can you blame me, my friend, to whom I have uttered the word *love*?

24 October 1968

A terminal case of stomach cancer in its final stage. In poor surgical conditions, I perform a probing operation and discover with great regret that the cancer has metastasized. It is impossible to do anything for the patient, so I resign myself to suturing the wound and watching death close upon him. This afternoon, standing at his bedside, I feel an ache in my heart as though it is being cut. He forces a smile as he talks to me, but the tears are filling his eyes. "I am not blaming anyone. You and other comrades in the clinic have tried your best to cure me, but the disease is incurable. Then let it be. If I stay here, my body will rest on the hill of myrtles[69] among comrades. If I go down to the plain, I will only be able to see my parents one more time, and then I will go into the ground alone." I stand quietly, at a loss for words. I feel extremely shameful and indignant. Any other clinic would have given up on him. Even with better medical facilities, one might be able to lengthen his life a little longer. Here, I am like a defeated soldier, hands raised, ready to be disarmed by the enemy.

26 October 1968

Don't ever demand too much in any matter. Is there anything without limits, Thuy? So think again, evaluate everything objectively, put yourself in each situation to see it all.

---

[69]Myrtle is a wild plant found in the hills of North Vietnam and the northern part of central Vietnam. In late spring, when the myrtle blooms, its flowers turn the hills violet. It is a romantic notion to be buried on a hill of myrtle.

1 November 1968

The atmosphere at the organization is becoming more cordial each day. Is it because I'm a Party member? Or is it because I've grown as a physician and as a cadre? Is it true that because I am a Party member, I have come back to live in the mother womb?

Last year's review cites the Duc Pho clinic's achievement as an example to the whole province for achieving the best results in treatments and other matters. And I am among those recognized. I have a part in this group victory.

Looking back, I realize I have no regrets. In the dry season of '67, I was steady and remained here despite all the obstacles facing me, a bourgeois female physician who was fresh out of school, practicing to be a commanding cadre. I have overcome those challenges. Let's improve my strengths, overcome my weaknesses, refuse to compromise good results, and strive hard in assignments to further my progress.

It's really strange, in the relentless rain pouring down on this dark forest, somehow a flower garden always appears in front of my eyes, glowing in the beautiful spring sunshine. The row of roses, lilies, chrysanthemums, and cherry blossoms are in full bloom. . . . I remember strolling with a dear beloved—a tender scene, long gone. Oh, Thuy!

When will the South know such beautiful seasons of blossoms?

Here bombs and deaths still weigh heavily upon people's lives.

Yesterday, there was a twenty-one-year-old man with wounds all over his body. He called my name as though I could save him, but all I could do was weep as I watched him die in my powerless hands.

I see it now: in the South, the flowers of victory and hero-ism are blooms of flesh and bones, of many young lives. I am walking in the center of the South, in the middle of that flower garden, my heart filling with so much admiration, pride, and immense pain when each flower falls. I have always loved flowers, but now with each step, my appreciation for the true beauty of FLOWERS has given me a deeper understanding of love, hate, and pride.

(You're also a beautiful flower, aren't you, my little brother?)

2 November 1968

Seeing my young brother's confidence shining through his letter, I feel bad about the letter I sent. It probably hasn't arrived. When it does, he certainly will be unhappy because of my questions. Oh, my young brother, forgive me. I have misjudged your very sincere and earnest love.

I receive many letters, each bearing adoration and kind thoughts. I am warm in a cradle of love.

3 November 1968

Peace has come to the North! The unjust sounds of bombs have fallen silent in our beloved North.[70] Oh! Joy illuminates sixteen million faces, but pain lingers in the smiles, for the South still

---

[70]In November 1968 the U.S. military temporarily halted its bombing campaign in North Vietnam.

suffers in fire and smoke. It remains in the vise of the vicious, roaring devils.

Today, Dad, Mom, and dear ones in the joyous North must be thinking of the South and me. Total happiness has not arrived, but be happy!

8 November 1968

Sitting next to you, my young brother, holding your warm hands, I am in anguish because there is no way for me to protect you. If you fall in this atrocious struggle . . . oh, my young brother! I will remember forever this moment, remember all my life your bright, affectionate eyes, your tender words. Oh, young brother, I am afraid. If you die, when will my pain subside? Each time you confess your love to me, I am shaken by a strange emotion.

Why can we, revolutionists, love each other so much? A love as deep and immense as the ocean, a love that surges like frothing waves, passionate, pure.

10 November 1968

Each day I have more opportunities to join in the various social activities. I am invited to the province-wide meeting for women and to the province-wide meeting for youths, but I cannot afford to go. There are unreasonable arrangements. Once more I understand people's jealousies better. There are still people unhappy at seeing their comrades advance.

The historic moments in a sister-brother relationship, in the life of a revolutionary—remember all your life, young brother.

11 November 1968

Why do I feel immensely sad when everybody departs? I cannot say. In fact, I very much regret that I cannot attend the meeting because I would have been able to hear, understand, and see many precious things, advantageous for my progress.

Why do I need to ask why? I want to analyze emotions very clearly, but in the end I can only conclude that in a farewell, there is an immense sadness, an immense longing, and a nagging worry in the heart.

These same days last year, when I left Pho Hiep, I was surprised to ask myself why our sister-brother relationship stirred my heart so deeply. Now I ask that question once again. There is only one answer: a revolutionary sentiment fills my heart, and it's enough to move me.

Oh, Thuy! Oh, this girl full of affection! Your eyes should not fill with tears, even if they are distilled from sadness. You should smile as though you always had a smile on your lips. Don't let someone find a sigh behind that smile. Twenty-five years old already, be steady and mature with that age.

12 November 1968

I don't know what made me open my old diary and those old letters from Nghia. I think about my love for that adopted young brother, wondering if my sentiments are intact and as intense as before. Yes, I still love Nghia deeply. I am certain that my love will stay unchanged forever. My love for Nghia is a fact that cannot be lost. But the excitement of beginnings has faded.

I reexamine my love because I want to ask myself if I am the sort of person who, having the new, forgets the old. Having Thuan, I seem to pour all my affection onto him, but looking back, I know I have also loved Nghia just as much in the beginning. I had the same strange longing when we were apart, the same earnest sense of waiting when he was absent. And yet Nghia is much like Thuan in the way he loves me, in both thought and action. Just the other day, I disagreed with Nghia in my refusal to accept his ring; now I have the same frustration with Thuan when he tries to give me money to buy a radio.

In my dissatisfaction, I have come to learn more about love. One cannot measure love with objects, but they are signs.

Oh, Thuy, how wonderful it is to be loved! Why do we have such intense emotions? I have no answer.

16 November 1968

How can I describe all the feelings we have for each other? Standing beside you, I am in bliss when you take my hand in yours and place in it all your love and trust. There are times when I cannot help thinking about us, our actions, and these intense, consuming emotions. Are these things we feel merely some sentiments born of our revolutionary zeal, the bonds of comrades, or the desperate thirst of lonely hearts, the bleeding hearts of this war? I can fathom no other cause—and yet I still feel so strange because of my boundless revolutionary heart.

21 November 1968

Every time I say good-bye to you, my young brother, I realize I love you even more. Hugging you in my arms, kissing your eyes, I feel that nothing can make us forget the hours and minutes we share. You have asked me many times why I love you. Why? It's because of your sufferings, because of your courage before tremendous dangers, and because your heart thirsts for love, but your life is lonely and cold. Of course you have the affection of our countrymen and comrades, but true love has eluded you. I come to you with admiration, with belief, and with a strange fondness. I do not say I love you more than everybody. As a big sister, I do not say I love you more than Nghia, more than Khiem, but I can say that I will cherish you forever with a boundless love.

You held my hand, saying passionately, "Believe me, believe that other than my late parents, no one has won or will win my love more thoroughly than you have."

I have asked you many times not to think that, but you're adamant about this unrealistic declaration. What can I say? Yes! I believe you, and I promise to try my best to repay your noble love.

Oh! My dear young brother, you are the bright fire that ignites the revolutionist's heart. It is a passion I have grasped only vaguely until now.

24 November 1968

Life spreads before us in a thousand pieces of love, pain, hope, and jealousy. Half of our heart is filled with red blood, half with black. In our mind there is also a balance between the bright, intelligent, and beautiful facets and the dark, negative, and cowardly parts.

If I can grasp that in its entirety, then I can achieve tranquillity and stability in this life.

Tonight I sit meditating by the late-burning lamp. I do not want to be sad, but sadness still comes to obscure my eyes. I wish I had a dear friend here to share my turmoil. If you were here, you would take my hand and kiss it in empathy. Isn't that so, my dear?

25 November 1968

So much work, headaches and exhaustion! I want nothing more than to return quietly to the comfort of love. But wishes are merely wishes, reality is always reality. The heartbreaking moans of patients haunt me still; difficult and frustrating work piles up before my eyes!

26 November 1968

It's my birthday,[71] and the sounds of the enemy's guns reverberate in all directions. I am used to helping wounded soldiers evade the enemy, wearing a heavy backpack on my shoulders. It's nothing. Two arduous years have hardened me to the bullets and the fire of war.

---

[71]Dang Thuy Tram was born on November 26, 1942.

The forest has gone peculiarly silent, the sounds of gunfire gone. Everyone is intently following the status of the battles.

As for me, I suddenly remember the peaceful days in the North—sunlight in winter, the warmth of great joy, Dad and Mom buying me flowers, having a party, friends coming to congratulate me. . . . Now my desires are different from those of the past. If I have those things, I should save them for those people who have risked death for the last twenty-three years, and for the adolescents growing up with suffering, hatred, and sacrifice. And for my dear friends in this land of the South. Oh, Dad and Mom, save your love for us, prepare to welcome me and all your sons from the South when we return. My young brothers will deserve your love.

27 November 1968

Sadness and longing weigh heavily upon my heart!

Oh, why is life so complex? I want to forget everything. I want only true love to calm my tumultuous heart. Why aren't you here, my young brothers?[72] With you by my side, we would need only silence, and you would understand and share my sadness.

29 November 1968

Criticism and counsel from the Party.[73]

---

[72]Thuy is referring to Nghia and Thuan.

[73]"Three Pro, Three Anti" criticism and self-criticism sessions were ubiquitous in Vietnamese communist organizations. Usually called *Kiem Diem* or "examining your points," they were a

STRENGTHS:

- persevering spirit, fearlessness in the face of danger, willingness to sacrifice, completion of assignments
- high organizational awareness
- amiable behavior, liked by people
- good understanding and concern for wounded soldiers
- good training work

WEAKNESSES:

- insufficient leadership and management skills
- still lack effectiveness in assignments, sometimes lead by getting the group's opinion
- still has bourgeois attitude
- still weak in guarding secrets and preventing fraud
- still weak in reviewing and pushing forth accomplishments

6 December 1968

I've been pondering my relationships with others, how I really appear in other people's eyes. People who haven't lived with me, but have only known me a short time or only interact with me through work (clinical treatment, training, and youth activities), all

---

regular part of Party meetings. When Ho Chi Minh was in China, the leadership in North Vietnam had developed a self-criticism program which it was about to launch about the time of Ho's return. Ho Chi Minh disagreed with the program as it existed because it only focused on self-criticism, just on the negative aspects of each person. It was Ho Chi Minh's recommendation that the criticism sessions stress and build on the strengths of each person, too. Using Ho's recommendation, the Three Positives/Three Negatives program was developed and implemented. At the time of Thuy's writing, both military personnel and civilians participated in the process.

like me. Those who have lived a long time beside me can be classified into three types:

- people who do not like me, and look for my weaknesses to criticize; they are few in number
- people who have a lot of affection for me, who love me with a special love and are always on my side; there are not too many of this type, but not too few, either.
- the majority, who love and hate me equally

What now, Thuy? What can I do with these relationships? How can I improve them? Who can satisfy everyone in this life?

7 December 1968

Seeing Thuong, I realize it has been a very long time since I was able to sit by him, talk with him as we did in the days on duty down on the plain. After a year apart, I am very happy that each of us has matured. And the sister-brother relationship has also grown, seasoned with time, become steady before winds and waves. Nurture that sentiment, little brother!

9 December 1968

It's a beautiful sunny afternoon on the road to the Party's school, the light streaming down through the tall treetops.

I am stirred by a sudden memory of the days I spent near you, young brother—the day we transported palm leaves, the day we arrived at the top of the hill, the day we sat in class. My affection gleams a pure, shiny color. Will it ever fade?

For me, a big sister . . . when I return to the North to live happily, will my affection for you sparkle the way it does now? And for you, young brother—will you be true to what you said in the last letter: "If I have a lover, I will tell her that my love for you, big sister, is higher than my love for her"?

16 December 1968

The problems are mounting, one after another. The enemy has started a major mopping-up operation.[74] Our area is in the path of their attack, so all programs have to be redirected. All of us are focused on reacting to the enemy's operation. One of our programs is the General Professional Conference,[75] whose purpose is to review the achievements of the last two years; I have been waiting for it with high expectations. Due to many reasons, the conference has been moved up, but today it's delayed because of the enemy. What a disappointment!

It's like what I say in the note sent to you this morning, young brother. When will I see you again? When can we fulfill our small but earnest wish? In your letter, you wrote, "Longing for you, my sister, fills my life." It's the same for me; longing and worry make me anxious all the time. I hope you will stand firm before all difficulties and dangers as always. I promise to hold you in my arms

---

[74]The American military called these maneuvers search-and-destroy missions.

[75]The district-level (which included provincial, village, and sub-village representatives) committee meetings were attended by party officials. During these meetings the Party Committee would establish objectives, evaluate strategies, and assign tasks.

when we meet again, and I will cover your eyes with kisses, with my undying love.

17 December 1968

The news of Duong's capture this second time is shockingly painful.

Just a few days ago I received his letter, a long letter in which he wrote about his deep affection for me and asked me to accept him as a young brother (that adopted-brother story again!). I disagreed with him because of many reasons: first, unlike Nghia, Thuong, and Thuan, Duong has not done anything to make me admire and love him as deeply; second, Duong still has characteristics that I do not expect from a dear one. For Duong I only have sympathy, understanding, and an appreciation of his deep affection for me.

Now Duong is captured again. Fresh out of prison—still not yet recovered from that saga—he has to weep for his father, shot by the Americans. His father's funeral was barely over before the enemy came again and killed his big brother in a tunnel, and captured Duong and took him away. They burned down his house. His mother is left to weep silently by her son's body, on the bare, charred ground of their burnt home. Is there anything more painful than that?

Oh, Duong, each time I remember you, my heart fills with hatred for the bandits robbing our nation, a hatred so powerful it's choking me. We must make them pay for their sins; we must avenge your sufferings and the deaths of countless comrades in this atrocious war.

18 December 1968

No, it could not be as Mui said; our path is one of friendship, not a road bright in the warm sunshine of love. Therefore, in the past, now and forever, I only consider Mui as an understanding, trusting, and affectionate friend. That is enough, Mui. We should not and cannot go further.

It's a small incident, but why am I sad? It's not one thing, but many small events that keep occurring daily. Life is so complex, something new happens each day in a different way. Oh, Thuy! If you want love and affection to have many facets, then how can you expect other things like sadness, anxiety, and people's jealousies to be simple?

Don't be sad. Laugh! Stand firm, no matter what happens. Hold intact forever your faith and the immense hope that you've kept in your soul for years.

Tonight I'm sitting on guard duty by the feeble glow of an oil lamp in a small house. The patients' moans make me strangely sad. More than ever, in this darkness, my yearnings surge like wild flames. Oh, my dear beloved, does anyone understand my heart tonight?

19 December 1968

I hike up to the top of a high mountain for a labor assignment. Gazing down the sweeping vista, I suddenly recognize, with a sense of unease, the beach of the South Wing of Duc Pho far in the distance before me. The fog shields the landscape, but many of its features are still familiar, the road 32, 33, of Quy Thien, the rows of houses close to the camp at the foot of Nui Dau[76] . . . so much warmth and love there, tender memories of the revolutionary life, hearts brooding over the precious love held for me. . . . It's only a piece of land in South Vietnam, and yet why do I feel so dearly bonded here?

21 December 1968

For a long time I haven't thought of M. . . . Today, rereading the letters from the North, letters from Thai,[77] Phuong, Uncle Hien[78] . . . I suddenly feel sorrow descending over me. Out there everyone hopes for my happiness, thinking that I am happy to see M. again. But why does life have so many ironies? Uncle Hien writes that Dung and he have overcome the rough patch in their relationship. Now, in Dung, he finds not only goodness, kindness, and stability, but also the profound love of a soul mate.

The joy and happiness of love have not come to me. I don't know what the future will bring, whom I will love, what that person will be like. Will my heart still be capable of true love?

Oh, Thuy! Are you pessimistic? Look around you, there are so many comrades, so many young men, who have sacrificed their youth for the revolution. They have fallen without ever finding happiness. Why do you think only of yourself? Don't look toward

---

[76]Nui Dau is a mountain southeast of Duc Pho, between the National Highway (Route One) and the coast. A cave in this mountain became a temporary clinic where Thuy administered first aid to wounded soldiers. The cave was less than a half-mile from the U.S. firebase known as Debbie.

[77]Vo Thi Thai was one of Thuy's best friends.

[78]The intimate name of Mr. Doan Que, Thuy's uncle and confidant.

the North, look around here; this land is still burning hot with suffering, bombs, and fire.

23 December 1968

Commemorating two full years away from home. Three o'clock in the afternoon, this same day two years ago, a truck[79] took me onto a different road. The road was extremely perilous; I knew that before embarking on it.

Yet today, after two years of reality, do you still grieve when you see thorns and spikes on that road, Thuy? What sufferings? This is life! There are flowers and sunshine, and there are dark clouds muddying up the sky. In the long length of a year, there are sunny days and rainy days.

This afternoon I know to set aside my frustrations and cheerfully hold up a book to teach. Tonight I know how to smile calmly before the reactions of a person whose rights were infringed. Then why now, beside the late-night lamp with a small notebook, am I brimming with tears? Don't cry, oh Thuy! Be calm and steady when you know you are right. If you must cry, hold your tears until you have a dear one's hand in yours; only then can you confess your frustrations. As for thorns and bitterness, dangers, and trials of life, I hope I can keep this smile I have been wearing for so long, although . . . hidden behind that smile are so many tears. Save them for your dear ones, are you listening, Thuy?

---

[79]Thuy left Hanoi in a truck accompanied by other civilians—photographers, filmmakers, painters, and medical personnel. After a week, Thuy walked another two and a half months, from the North, until reaching her assigned destination in Quang Ngai Province.

26 December 1968

I receive letters from M. and his father. Almost everyone who knows our story is happy for me.[80] And yet I am deeply saddened.

M.'s father says I am right on many points: the revolutionary and bold sentiments, the faithful love of a girl. But he fails to see two things in me: self-respect and pride. If I understood at the beginning the differences between my soul and the soul of that soldier, then perhaps I would not have loved him. Just the imbalance between the depths of our feelings would have been enough to push aside the love I yearn for.

Ten years, the road has not been short. Now I am at a fork, turning onto another road. Nobody knows where it leads.

Therefore, there is nothing to be joyful about. He is still the M. I met the other day, but now I am a person who has seen life and has matured. The joyful, bubbly love of those innocent days long ago is gone.

Holding M.'s letter, I don't read it right away. And after reading it, I feel extremely sad. A few hours later, I calmly returned to work unperturbed, as if nothing has happened. Oh, Thuy! Has your heart become dry, drained of emotions?

31 December 1968

New Year's Eve, the night sky is clear, not a trace of cloud. It's very late, but nobody feels sleepy. Conversations resonate in all the

---

[80]It is possible that Thuy is referring to the fact that people are happy, knowing that she and M. are working near each other in Quang Ngai.

houses. Nobody wants to sleep because tomorrow another journey begins.

After this grand meeting, each of us will go in a different direction; each will receive a difficult assignment in the coming days. The struggle has become more and more dangerous in this final period. Blood must still be shed. Shed in copious amounts to secure a decisive victory.

Sitting by my young brother's side, I cannot say the things I need to say. There are too many other people around us. I am a little sad because we cannot realize all the things we desire; however, I understand you when I see your eyes, when I hear your low sigh. Dear young brother, love gives us faith, strength, and the joy of reunion, then, of course, it will also give us longing when we are apart. Therefore, why are you sad? Smile, my young brother. When will I see you again? Will I ever see you again? I don't want to follow that pessimistic thought.

Good-bye, my young brother. I hold you in my arms, listening to your breath, wanting to say many things, but I stay silent because I believe you understand me, you know the deep, immense love I reserve for you.

1 January 1969

A new year begins! Chairman Ho wishes:

Last year we were victorious
This year greater victories are assured at the battlefront.
For independence—for freedom
Fight until the Americans leave, fight until the puppets fall.

Advance soldiers, compatriots
North and South reunified, no other spring more joyous.

This New Year's Day lacks the excitement and enthusiasm that filled the previous New Year's Day. Is my view colored by my limited awareness, by my inappropriate evaluation of all the achievements? Or isn't it? Is it because last year has the joy of "a new beginning" and this year there is only a sense of continuation? (I am talking about the public sentiment here, not just my own.)

4 January 1969

Lying next to Ninh, listening to her story, I wonder why she suddenly tells me all her feelings for "third brother."[81]

The things Ninh reveals about Thuan make me very repentant. I love Thuan, thinking that I have understood him all this time, but my insights are only glimpses of his true self.

I did not comprehend all the facets of devotion to duty, responsibility, and conscience of a very noble medical soldier like him. In the general report on common achievements, Thuan has three brief lines to describe them. In fact, I did not know there had been stormy nights when he rushed to his duty despite the bombs exploding all around him. Once Ninh felt bad about

---

[81] Ta Thi Ninh, a cousin to Thuan, was a nurse who worked with Thuy. Ninh kept a traditional medicinal garden that she started when she and Thuy worked together. Here Ninh tells Thuy about her feelings for Thuan, whom she calls "Third Brother." South Vietnamese often use the order between siblings in place of a real name as a way to show respect and also intimacy. Thuan was the second child of his parents; therefore he was called "Third." In central and South Vietnam, the title *Ca,* which means "First," is reserved for the village headman.

Thuan's heavy workload and decided to call another nurse instead of him. When he discovered her good intentions, Thuan vehemently scoffed at her decision, demanding that from then on she must alert him of all cases even if he was sleeping, sick, or preoccupied with other tasks.

I know so little about his anguish over the deaths in his family. Seeing him going about his days calm and cheerful, I have been oblivious that there are long nights when he does not sleep but weeps like a child. I haven't known about the times he scolded Cho for not taking care of his own family, Cho cried, and Thuan cried with her.

I know so little about Thuan's needs. I trust his strength so much it hasn't occurred to me that he suffers in silence, holding his needs in check so that the rest of us can have more. He is weaving a hat to sell for some pocket money. . . . Oh! Why am I so shallow? I haven't even fully grasped his feelings toward me.

Young brother! Big sister has mistreated you. How can I correct this? Your life is a lesson I will keep forever. I will honor the courage, the sacrifice, the spirit of responsibility, the altruism, the will, and the true sentiment of your revolutionist heart.

9 January 1969

Bon is twenty-one this year, twenty-one years, with seven battle injuries. This young scout-platoon leader has made an unforgettable impression on me.

The first time I saw Bon, he was admitted into the clinic with a minor injury in his leg. After a few days he left, even though his wound was not fully healed. Over a month later, I readmitted him at the clinic. This time the wound was in his shoulder. He had lost a lot of blood, so he was very tired and pale. When he regained consciousness after the surgery, a playful smile bloomed again on his pale lips. It was a very painful injury, but he did not whine or moan. He worried about one thing: being able to continue fighting. During my visits with him in the patients' ward, I often brushed his hair with my fingers and whispered to him: Don't worry, little brother. You can certainly still hold a gun well enough to fight the enemy.

Another day, I saw Bon in a marching troop, an AK-47[82] on his shoulder. He saw me from afar and shouted cheerfully, "Greetings, Doctor! Report to Doctor: My arm is as good as new!" He waved his arm to show that the joint functioned normally. I laughed happily when I saw the healthy hue on his cheeks and the playful grin on the face of that liberation soldier.

Today, Bon is back at the clinic again, very pale. He lies motionless and silent, without a single moan. His leg is lacerated, mauled by a mine, his clothes soaked with blood. With love, the other comrades and I try our utmost to treat him.

After the amputation of his leg, Bon smiled and said, "Now survival is eighty percent certain."

---

[82]The AK-47 assault rifle was the basic infantry weapon for both the North Vietnamese Army and the Liberation forces in South Vietnam during the Vietnam War. Though of Russian design, most of the weapons used in Vietnam were built in the People's Republic of China. In the early years of the war, some U.S. military soldiers considered the AK-47 superior to their own weapon, the Colt M-16. The original M-16 was difficult to keep clean in humid jungle conditions, and it was prone to jamming when fired in full automatic mode. Consequently, U.S. soldiers occasionally took AK-47s from dead enemy soldiers and used them, in spite of the fact that the weapon's distinctive "popping" sound in combat tended to draw fire from their own forces.

In private, I still worry because Bon lost so much blood. His pulse is very fast (140 to 150)—but I am hopeful.

In the end, he cannot survive. Having lost so much blood, he lacks the strength to recover. Oh, Bon, your blood has crimsoned our native land, flowing down the length of the road to battle. Your heart has stopped so that the heart of the nation can beat forever.

Bon dies, his eyes closing gently as if to sleep. Sitting by his side, brushing his hair, I think he is still with us. Then my tears fall onto his hair. No! Don't die! You will live forever in my heart and in the hearts of your comrades who have fought at your side in this life-and-death struggle.

Sadness floods over me. Hatred for the invaders presses down a thousand times more heavily upon my heart. Looking at his lifeless body, I am bewildered by the thought of the losses and sufferings that the dear young brothers must endure in their fight against the enemy, day and night, through bombs and bullets. In the last few days the enemies have been attacking Pho Cuong mercilessly. Thuan nearly died several times. . . . Oh! We will still suffer as long as those bloodthirsty foes remain here. There is no other way but to crush the heads of those vicious dogs.

10 January 1969

A sadness as persistent as the incessant rain of the past ten days, days as long as months. There is yearning and restlessness inside me. I am plagued with worries and sorrows. I always see dangers threatening my dear ones in this struggle. What can I say? . . . A day shadowed by the American bandits is a day of pain and death. Oh, this vendetta, when can it be paid?

11 January 1969

Life in Pho Cuong remains arduous. The enemy continues the sweeping pattern of destruction, sacking villages, burning houses, and seizing peasants' rice stores in an attempt to implement their pacification plan quickly. There is still gunfire in that direction. Each shot reminds me of the folks down there, making me empathize with their plight. And in the midst of those million images, I see you clearly, Thuan, your simple black attire drenched with sweat and rain. Exhaustion is plain on your gaunt face, but your eyes are gleaming, a smile lingering on your lips. Missing you, I saw traces of you everywhere, in the unruly hair of the young liberation soldier who died in my arms, in Lien who is burdened with death and pain.

Lien has just learned that her mother is dying alone. There is no one else at home. Her older brother regrouped to the North.[83] One of her sisters went to Saigon. Her fifth sister-in-law was shot and injured by the enemy, who then carried her away somewhere. The old mother stayed behind at home, enduring loneliness and privation to spiritually support her daughter Lien, who has joined the Resistance in the South. Now the old mother is stricken with a brain hemorrhage, lying unconscious in bed, in a cold, empty house. There is no one to care for her. Lien cries, her tears permeating my heart as thoroughly as your tears had the day you wept for your father.

Each one of these tragedies has been caused by the devil bandits. There is no argument about that.

---

[83]When the Geneva Accords temporarily divided the country in 1954, many South Vietnamese "regrouped" by going to North Vietnam.

12 January 1969

Binh comes up from the lowlands to inform us about the Americans' withdrawal. The situation at Pho Cuong has returned to normal. Through your letter, I learn that you are well. In the four pages, you only say you are too tired to write the last sentence; the rest are just longing and worries for me. You have eaten one meager meal a day for the last ten days, your clothes keep getting wet, and you could not change. Tanks and soldiers chase you. You skirted death several times. . . . You have never told me any of that. I only learn through your letters to other people. I feel and worry for you, but I am also frustrated with you. I want to be angry with you for your lack of sincerity (for not telling me about your hardships). But in the end, I know it's because you do not want me to worry; it's nothing other than what you once called "a deep and strange love that is impossible to explain to you."

14 January 1969

The whole house is empty. The clinic is silent and oddly somber. There are only a few wounded soldiers and some staff left. I can hear the murmurs of the stream outside.

I am already twenty-six years old, no longer a naïve girl. Why do I let this gloomy scene color my feelings? In fact, it's the other way around. Nguyen Du[84] says, "When one is sad, the scenery can

---

[84]Thuy quotes *The Tale of Kieu,* an epic poem in Vietnamese written by the eighteenth-century writer Nguyen Du (1766–1820), widely regarded as the most significant work of Vietnamese literature. In 3,254 verses, written in *luc bat* (6/8) meter, the poem recounts the life of Thuy Kieu, a young woman who chose to sacrifice herself to save her family. *The Tale of Kieu* was written under a pseudonym because it criticized aspects of the Confucian moral order.

never be cheery." What joy is there when the American bandits are trampling on our nation and killing our countrymen? What joy is there when our country is still divided, when family members are still scattered in all directions?

But, Thuy, does your heart recognize only yearnings and sorrows? Our struggle demands that the people have great joy and a strong will and belief in our cause. Nurture these positive sentiments and wipe away the cloud of sadness from your eyes.

16 January 1969

Nghia came to visit, but I was away grading student exams. My young brother left a letter and gifts for me.

Handing the gifts and money to me, Sister Ba says, "Such an adopted brother! That's precious!"

Sister Ba probably has no hidden thoughts, but I feel a bit uneasy. Perhaps she and many other people cannot and will not totally understand the noble sentiments between people whose hearts are full of effervescent affections, like me, Nghia, Thuan, Khiem, and Thuong. . . . We love each other with a miraculous love, a love that makes people forget themselves and think only of their dear ones. With that love, people can sacrifice their lives to protect their loved ones. Money and material gifts are meaningless if we don't see all the affection invested in those gifts. Do not evaluate a gift's material worth, but rather its sentimental value. Many times my young brothers have been in need of money to buy cigarettes, but still, when possible, they give me all their money. Sometimes my young brothers have hidden their needs to let me have what I need.

I must strive to deserve my young brothers' love.

18 January 1969

Reading your letter, I empathize with you, and I sit here and laugh alone. Your love is strange, immensely sincere, and vibrant. I have never read such a simple and candid letter. In each of those unpolished sentences, I discover even more about your very true heart. You worry from the smallest details to the biggest things; you worry if my future lover would be kind or cruel. . . . Those are very funny thoughts. I don't know what concept of love you have in order to imagine such a pitiful wife. That's right; you did not know my standards for a lover—the standards of an educated girl grown up in socialism. Don't worry little brother, my young brother! Your big sister is never easy in choosing a lover.

19 January 1969

It's a Sunday afternoon in the middle of the old forest, resplendent with clear sunshine and brisk wind. The radio is playing an international music program. . . . Working in a small room, I feel at peace in this scene. I forget the bombs, bullets, and fire, the deaths and suffering. Only an immense inspiration from the music remains in my heart.

I don't know whether I am worthy of blame or praise. I should be blamed for forgetting the constant sufferings of the people, for forgetting the crimes of the bloodthirsty devils trampling our nation. But I am worthy of praise because amid so much suffering, my heart is still optimistic with belief and with the vigor for life. Hope remains fresh and green in my soul.

Dear Phuong, you always feel the pain of separation within

each Vietnamese family. Here I see those aching scenes a thousand times more clearly. However, I still hope you and I won't lose the joy, the dream in our hearts. Let's still be as we were in the old days, young sister. Together again, we will listen to the international music program[85] each Sunday afternoon, we will scribble in our diaries, and our lives will still be full of dreams despite the bombs and bullets, the fire and smoke surrounding us.

22 January 1969

The nursing class is over. The students are going home. Many are hugging me. They feel a bond to me and are unwilling to let go. Their kisses on my cheeks are hot with affection, especially Ninh's. The little girl holds my hand and whispers sadly, "I'm going home, big sister." I don't know why she rests her head on my shoulder and cries. I've seen many tears, yet somehow the tears of this little sister moved me so much. Is it because I empathized with her? Her home was burned. There is not a grain of rice left to eat. Is it because I empathize with her for the many times she confided her heart to me? Is it because she also loves and cares for her third brother with deep affection? Perhaps it is because of all those things.

OK, return to your home, little sister. I wish you a steadfast journey on the victorious and difficult road of a health-care revolutionist.

---

[85]The international music program may have been playing classical music, a love of Thuy's father. When Thuy studied as a medical resident under her father, a well-regarded surgeon who remained in Hanoi, he often played classical music to relax after operations. A man with a strong interest in the arts, he preferred classical pieces featuring the violin. He played the violin at home, and urged his four daughters to learn to play the instrument and read music. Thuy played both the violin and the guitar.

7 February 1969

I spend the night in the house of an old widow. Is it the kitchen's flickering fire or my passion that makes it hard to sleep and easy to forget the cold of the mountain forest outside? A sharp pain shoots through me when I hear you say, "Big sister, if I should die without saying my last words to you, consider that I have said them today."

Hugging you, I have a frantic fear that the war will not spare anyone, that even you may fall while fulfilling your duties. Then . . . what can I do, young brother?

Will my sigh speak to you of all my worries and affection for you?

8 February 1969

Completed a period of hardship: fourteen days of climbing mountains, of crossing torrents, of rain, sun, and fog. During this trial, I am always happy because I am surrounded by loving friends. From a comrade I have never met before to a passerby, each person does his best to help me and the Duc Pho team.

I'm so happy the people of Duc Pho consider me one of them and share with me the joy and the pride of their heroic land.

I'm so pleased that the whole conference seems to hold the people of Duc Pho in the highest regard, giving them priorities and the highest honors. And I, a Hanoi girl from Duc Pho, am also a part of it.

What else, Thuy? Can this be the joy that has been growing since the hard old days and the happiness of living with my dear friends? The dear friends . . . the seasoned cadres who met me only once but already understood me; a young cadre, fresh out of school, trying her best to achieve; the diligent and sweet female friend who cares for others more than herself; and the young brother who loves me. He loves me with a strange affection. He takes care of everything for me, from a bowl of rice to a cup of water. After ten days living beside him, I ask myself, "How can there be such a love?" You and I, we both know it is a love between a sister and a brother, pure and sincere.

Is there anything we need to overcome, young brother?

I should answer that question myself before asking him.[86]

11 *February 1969*

Oh, Thuy, why is your troubled sleep filled with flickering images? Work piles up around you, waiting for resolution, but you still cannot forget—sentiment should always be guided by reason. Thuy, you must never let sentiment be separated from reason. Therefore . . . put away the longings that are burning in your heart to focus on your tasks, stow away the bright feelings bubbling in your lively heart. Are you listening, Thuy? Out there, the guns have announced a great, victorious spring.

---

[86]Thuy is questioning whether their love has any overtures of romance, anything beyond the sister-brother relationship. In wartime, people who were in danger developed affection for others in the same situation. This type of love or affection was not necessarily driven by sexual or romantic inclination.

14 February 1969

I celebrate the New Year (Tet)[87] with an army unit from the North. Many faces and voices remind me of the days in the North. Somehow sadness clenches my heart. Instead of staying longer to talk, I excuse myself and then walk home slowly. The afternoon sunlight has drained from the top of the hill; a cold breeze sighs. . . . An immense sadness and longing make me stop.

Tet has arrived, my third Tet away from home. Instead of being used to the loneliness of living in an unfamiliar land, instead of feeling cheered by the warmth and friendship of the folks of Duc Pho and Quang Ngai, I still feel as though it were my first day here, when I was just starting out. My only true wish is to live with Mom and Dad in our warm family nest, and feel that I am still a little girl wanting to be pampered, to be spoiled like a child by Mom, just like when I was her innocent little girl.

I want to write and tell you all this, but perhaps it is not necessary.

15 February 1969

Giao Thua,[88] the transition to the new year!

Is it *Giao Thua* already? Let it be the transition from the days of sufferings and fire to the days of peace and happiness. The nation is

---

[87] Tet is a period ranging from seven to ten days at the beginning of the lunar new year. It is considered an event in itself rather than merely the beginning of another year. For the Vietnamese, Tet is the most important holiday of the year, when families pay tribute to their ancestors at the ancestral grave sites and pray for good fortune in the coming year.

[88] *Giao Thua* refers to "the turning over of time, from the old year to the new year."

silent, but secretly roiling with preparations. Isn't this transition similar to that of giving birth, going from a heavy pregnancy to having a big, healthy baby?

Tonight, after an operation, I am so overwhelmed with fatigue and sorrow that I do not yearn for anything. Apathy is unworthy of you, Thuy!

17 February 1969

Young brother, you come because of your tasks, and certainly also because of me. I can see it clearly in your face. You and I, young brother and big sister, are alike: Tet belongs to others. For us, it's only a time of loneliness. I am far from home, far from the dear ones in both parts of the country—and you, young brother, you don't have anyone other than your two younger siblings. You have me, but I don't live near you.

That's fine. Love will warm our hearts.

Be joyful, young brother. Don't be sad when we are apart. I wish you a year full of luck, full of victories, and I wish that our relationship might grow ever stronger in time.

19 February 1969

It's terribly calm today. The southeastern wind of yesterday has vanished somewhere. The forest has settled into complete stillness, not a single leaf stirs. It seems the folks have also fallen silent, affected by the forest. They're working quietly at their tasks. I cannot read their thoughts, their faces are so serious, not a smile.

But within me lies an emotional chaos, longing for home, longing for you. And there are the old images from the good part of my life: a morning on the move, the same silent forest of tall trees, the same bright and rosy light on top of a mountain . . . a morning in the plains, sunlight cutting through the bamboo and falling onto the table behind the window. . . .

There are powerful yearnings . . . yearning for what I do not know, yearning for everyone to return, yearning for time to pass quickly so new, joyful days can come . . . these are vague things, and yet they pester my soul.

And it seems there is a shade of regret in my worries. If the things we fear come to pass, I am ready to die for the final victory. The coming responsibility is so huge I do not want to face reality, for I will see only doubts and impasses. Let it be, I will resolve whatever comes. I am usually calm in difficult situations, am I not? However, I must prepare and plan ahead.

20 February 1969

The tasks are heavier than ever. I have never been as worried as I am now. The coming responsibility demands extraordinary professional, organizational, and leadership skills. I have gained a great deal of experience, but the demands threaten to drown me beneath their sheer weight. What can I do? I can only try, try, and try. That's all!

That soldier has probably already departed for the battlefront. I wish you a victorious return so I can see again your shiny dark eyes, your face, the face of a liberation soldier.[89]

---

[89]In all likelihood, Thuy is referring to M.

21 February 1969

Reading a poem from the North. P.H.[90] wrote it as a present to me:

> There is the sky where you live
> In the past and also in the future
> Where a small love is nurtured, a sparrow's nest
> The little bird flew away . . .

Isn't it true that an unfulfilled love is still alive in you, the artist? To me, your face is shielded by others from long ago, but after reading your poem today, I suddenly miss you.

That summer the flame trees[91] bloomed red in the streets, the sun shining brightly through the green canopy. I was returning home from school, passing by the three-story house on 14 Le Truc Street.[92] Looking up, I saw you standing alone waiting for me, your hair falling over sad eyes.

That afternoon a storm howled, wind blowing dust in all directions. You waited for me at the beginning of Hang Day Street.[93] I rode my bike past, surprised to recognize you under the city light. . . . I never loved you, my feelings for you were those of a friend. Your love was shattered after my many refusals, but you still loved me.

In your last letter, you say, "You should go, then, you will meet

---

[90]P.H. stands for Le Phu Huong, a friend of Thuy's from their early teenage years.

[91]The flamboyant poinciana, known as the "flame tree" in English, blooms with beautiful red flowers.

[92]Le Truc Street is in Hanoi, near Doi Can Street.

[93]A street in Hanoi.

a worthy lover, but I can say with certainty that there is no one in this life who loves you like I do."

It seems what you say is true, but I do not regret because I don't love you in that way. How can we have a beautiful and fair love? Anyway, I understand you very well. Please believe that I will repay your love with the love of a little sister, my brother.

24 February 1969

Fighting broke out the night before last. Determined, we waited to vent our rage through the barrels of our guns.

All at once, my heart became restless with both joy and worries. Perhaps it was because of my responsibility; my tasks are very heavy. And what else? Wasn't it a painful apprehension in my heart? Which of my dear ones in the line of fire will fall in this fight?

Of course, there must be sacrifices for victory.

What else can you say, Thuy?

26 February 1969

A spring night, the moon is strangely clear. I want to put away the intense feelings in my heart and focus on work, but it's impossible. I don't know what can possibly drain my heart of longings, dreams, and hopes. Last year, even in an underground chamber, hearing the sounds of the enemy searching for us above, I still told Khiem Pavel's[94] story. In the middle of the enemy's operation, bombs and

---

[94] A character in *How the Steel Was Tempered.*

bullets fell around me as I sat inside a crack in the mountain and wrote my letters and diary. Now, beneath this mountain of work, I am still a person with a soul burning for life.

In fact, it's not my love for a certain young man that makes me feel and act the way I do. This is something immense and vibrant within me. My longings extend to many people, from one person to another, from a niece whom I have never met, to a little sister struggling in her duties who always calls me "second sister." How I miss the dear young brother who threw himself into work but reserved his heart for me. This morning I stood by the table of a young wounded soldier with black eyes and long lashes. Seeing him made me remember the day that I sat gazing at you.

What am I? I am a girl with a heart brimming with emotions, yet with a mind that never falters before a complex and dangerous situation.

3 March 1969

After doing my rounds in the patients' ward, I return to my room in the middle of the night and lie restless, unable to sleep. The jungle is very quiet, not a sound, no bird's cry, falling leaves, or branches shaking in the wind.

What are you thinking, oh, Thuy? What thoughts keep your eyes open, staring into this darkness?

In the pale moonlight I see many beautiful and fond visions from the days living in the land of Duc Pho. But then the memories of separations and sufferings come. . . .

Oh, Thuy, you should blame yourself! Don't you hear the

moans of the wounded, the guns in the distance? The battlefield is still in a victorious season.

6 March 1969

Each time I read these tender letters, I fathom yet another depth of my young brother's love for me. I'm coming to understand its fullness. What can I say? What can I do to deserve his love? In my eyes, he is like Nghia, Thuong, and Khiem—soul-mate brothers.

There have always been others closer to my heart.

And yet, in every letter, in every minute, he keeps repeating one sentence: "Only you, my sister, I love more than anyone else in my life."

What can I say, young brother?

9 March 1969

Seeing brother Tan again, my heart suddenly becomes unsettled. Is this from the sorrow, the longing, or the blame for M.? I don't know for certain. I only feel an unusual disturbance in my heart. Tan has stirred long-forgotten memories—memories blurred by both time and intention.

Oh, M.! Where are you? Tan returns without news of you. Are we truly separated?

Why do I still feel my heart bleeding? Why is a wound in the heart so hard to heal?

This afternoon, here and at your place, together we organize for a large-scale attack. In that preparation, we both are there, participating in the struggle. And yet . . . why do we feel so far apart, my beloved comrade?

11 March 1969

Those liberation soldiers are so admirable. They are strong and courageous on the battlefronts. And here on their sickbeds they are extremely strong and courageous, too.

There is a cadre with an extraordinary capacity for pain. Eyes brimming with tears, he still manages a smile and says, "It's nothing." Sitting at his side, holding his feverish hand and listening to his irregular breathing, I empathize with him, but do not know what to say. Besides my physician's compassion, I also feel a friendship with him because we both come from the same place. I do not want to reveal this so I just smile at him.

There is the liaison boy with a dimple on his cheek, smiling constantly despite the painfully inflamed wound on his arm.

There is a severely injured cadre. His hand is battered and torn, and yet he still smiles optimistically.

Today you are on a military movement again, a victorious excursion. I wish all of you a victorious departure. Please send my greetings to the soldier with the shining black eyes.

12 March 1969

What can I think about the change in Nghia's feelings toward me?

A betrayal?

That word sounds too heavy, but, truthfully, that's how I feel. I have discovered a crack in my affection for Nghia. How sad!

Did you forget all your promises? What did the four of us, sister and brothers, say that night on the Beach of Pho Hiep? The letters, the gifts you sent with your entire heart in them . . .

Now! Answer me, my young brother. Have you detached yourself from my affection?

Suddenly I think of Thuan. Could Thuan change like that someday? If he does, I will be very frustrated. I won't be able to trust anyone again.

13 March 1969

Another comrade sacrificed his life. The wound went all the way through his abdomen. His condition was not good after the operation, and worsened over time. Perhaps there was an internal hemorrhage caused by some undiscovered shrapnel cutting a vein. After a joint diagnosis, the common opinion was not to perform a second operation. Privately, I hesitated. In the end he died.

I developed a severe headache, thinking about his death. Why did he die? Was it because of my indecision? Very probably. If I had been decisive, he might have had a ten percent chance of survival. I conformed to the majority's opinion and dropped something worth doing.

He died with a small notebook in his breast pocket. It held many pictures of a girl with a lovely smile and a letter assuring him of her steely resolution to wait for his return. On his chest, there was a little handkerchief with the embroidered words *Waiting for you.*

Oh, that girl waiting for him! Your lover will never come back; the mourning veil on your young head will be heavy with pain. It will mark the crimes committed by the imperialist killers and my regret, the regret of a physician who could not save him when there was a chance.

16 March 1969

Correction and Education from the Party: A Study of the Three-Construction, Three-Counteraction Plan.[95]

Contributing ideas from the Party sub-branch:

STRENGTHS:

- significant progress in leadership, full comprehension of duties, covering all aspects of work
- completion of heavy tasks assigned by superior
- persistent standpoint, high awareness of organization
- careful planning with supervision and stipulation

WEAKNESSES:

- sometimes still lacking thoroughness in work
- did not use all investigative capabilities to draw experience from treatments
- still weak in improving the staff's living conditions

---

[95]The Three-Construction Plan was a campaign to motivate the population, generate new ideas, and acquire self-sufficiency in the production of food. The Three-Counteraction Plan involved measures to deal with natural disasters, plague, and famine.

17 March 1969

Reading your brief letter filled with both love and displeasure, I suddenly feel the tenderness of the old days reviving in my heart—the days when our relationship was whole.

I can't remember if I had thought carefully about that reply I gave you: "What happened in the last nine years cannot easily be forgotten, even though everyone wants to forget. We each have our own opinion, but the public also has an opinion about us. Still, I know the roots of my love still lie deep within my heart, dormant but not dead. It can sprout, it can grow if spring returns. A part of me is still that young girl you know, the one who loves to feel cool raindrops on her face."

19 March 1969

Last night we attacked Duc Pho district seat. The whole area burned under the furious gunfire from our soldiers. Luc, a wounded cadre who had just recovered enough to fight, was among those courageous soldiers. He fell in the first attack. Hearing the news, I felt an enormous ache. I could still see clearly his youthful, intelligent eyes and courageous face.

Luc often had a red scarf on his shoulder. I could still see the words stitched on his scarf: "Pledge Firmly to Sacrifice for the Nation's Survival."

I could still hear his voice singing in the afternoon, "Oh, mountain and river, how beautiful, when the moon lights the hills, clouds fly beneath the feet. . . ."

Oh, Luc, have you died?

Your voice still reverberates in my ears. The ink on your letter is still fresh. You are like Bon, Khiem, and all the heroes who fell for tomorrow's victory. You live forever in my heart and the hearts of all our people.

21 March 1969

I need to reexamine my behavior. It seems everybody finds me approachable and amiable when they first meet me. Could this be the reason I have become biased in some instances? There are times when I speak without tact. It is right to be frank, but it is wrong to abandon subtlety.

Try to change, oh, Thuy!

25 March 1969

I haven't had an opportunity to come down to the lowlands for over a year now. Somehow, these days, my wish to go down there burns hot like the summer sun. I miss the lowlands, covered with green rice fields thick with grain-heavy stalks, dotted with colored dresses and white hats of pretty girls. Oh, the lowlands! The fire of war still burns red, but the green fields of life still rise from the earth.

Dear young brother, I miss you, surprisingly. I wish so much to see you again, to look into your cherished eyes, to hold you in my arms, to kiss you the way I kiss my kinfolk's child.

27 March 1969

I hear that the Area[96] General Hospital[97] wants me back. It's only a rumor, but I feel deeply sad. If it is indeed an order, I must obey. I cannot protest. But, oh! I can't say enough about my sadness. Am I going to leave this place? Moving to the province headquarters is far enough, but moving to the zone . . . When can I see my dear ones again?

Is there anywhere like this land? This land has nurtured me with affections and challenges, trained me to mature in the face of suffering, and made me a solid cadre.

I receive your letter full of longings and worries for me. You don't know that I will have to leave—we won't turn weak at farewell, the two of us, sister and little brother, will we? But it's difficult for you just to say good-bye to go a short way down to the village. How can I say good-bye to go all the way to the zone, brother?

2 April 1969

The enemies are pouring into Dong Ram,[98] less than thirty minutes from here. We organize ourselves to evade their operation again.

---

[96]The North Vietnamese Military Command divided South Vietnam into strategic zones, which it called "areas." Here Thuy is referring to Area V, which consisted of the provinces Quang Nam, Quang Ngai, Binh Dinh, Phu Yen, and Khanh Hoa. At the time of this entry, the seat of Area V was in the mountain district of Tra My, Quang Nam. The U.S. military divided up South Vietnam into "corps." In U.S. military terminology, Thuy was working in "I Corps."

[97]Thuy was assigned to a civilian Public Health System under the direction of the NLF. Thuy's clinic, a small hospital, served soldiers and civilians who lived in the battle area. Most of the locations where Thuy practiced medicine were in "free-fire zones," which meant that the policy of the American forces allowed them to fire on any Vietnamese in the area because they were deemed to be either enemy soldiers or collaborators. Thuy's clinic had no protective immunity under the U.S. military directive.

[98]Dong Ram, a hamlet southwest of the town of Duc Pho, was about a thirty-minute walk from Thuy's clinic.

Tonight our clinic prepares for the arduous task in silence. I'm not sure why I feel profoundly compassionate toward my wounded comrades. With their wounds still unhealed, they will have to climb mountain after mountain to evade the enemy. Their injuries are fresh and painful, but they will have no rest.

As long as the American bandits remain in our land, there will be suffering—nothing has changed!

5 April 1969

If you knew how much I yearned for you, you would be here today, sitting next to me, holding my hand in silence.

Without a word, you would understand everything we want to say to each other.

Rain is pouring down.

I am cold and so sad—do you know this, my dear young brother?

6 April 1969

Why is that? Why am I not ecstatic to see you again after so many days of yearning?

Missing you has swept over me like a river on a monsoon day.

Why do my sadness and uneasiness hold me back from rushing to you and showering you with the pure love that you deserve?

I'm afraid of what they will think of us, afraid that they might misunderstand our noble love, this very innocent but very complex devotion. I know it is a pure love. Its complexity is what concerns me. Why do I have these concerns when my heart is as clear as a mirror?

There is really nothing to speculate about when you hold my hand and kiss it in love and respect, but I am still worried that people will misunderstand our affection. Oh, young brother, of course, we have done nothing to violate our friendly love, but I want to protect it. I don't want to give anyone a chance to say anything bad about our love, so don't blame me for being a little distant, for not treating you like close kin from day to day.

Do you understand, my young brother? My peculiar brother, intelligent, courageous, amiable, and admirable.

7 April 1969

I am overwhelmed with joy at receiving so many letters. Letters from Mom, from young brother, from people at the zone, in the province, district, and village—they all send me their warm thoughts and love. Their praises made me happy: "liked by everybody, loved by friends, trusted by the Party," "truly educated in all respects."

I don't know how many times I have asked myself what I must do to deserve everyone's trust.

Brother Tan's[99] letter also makes me think. He tells me about himself, then asks me, "It's up to you to decide whether I am distant or close to you. Do you think that I deserve to be your dear big brother or not?"

---

[99]Tan held the rank of secretary, the top communist official, in Duc Pho District. Thuy and Tan were extremely close. Tan survived the war, and named his daughter after Thuy. Thuy accepted Tan, the secretary of the District Board, as her big brother.

I admire you, brother, and I like you very much. It's not because you are the secretary of the District Board. I want you to lead and teach me like a caring big brother. It's just that I don't want people to think I am an easy girl, one who gives her heart readily, or that I want to have relationships with high-level officials.

8 April 1969

The enemy draws near the irrigation gutter.[100] Just a little closer and they would have seen our clinic and destroyed it. Knowing that the enemy is practically at my elbow, I somehow stay strangely calm.

After taking the wounded to the hiding place, I return to the clinic and stand in the operating room. I want to try to see if I have the courage and vigilance to resolve things like others who often stayed behind to defend the evacuation.

But in the end, the enemy did not come, and that night I slept soundly in the empty room amid the chaos left by our quick evacuation.

9 April 1969

I attend the meeting of our District Committee of Youth. My ideas are appreciated and discussed by other comrades. I regret that I have been too busy with many tasks, and cannot contribute more to the youth activities.

I do not know why I am comparing my position in the conference today with that of my role as a big sister when I played

---

[100]Split bamboo was used for rain gutters and also for conduits to provide water to the clinic.

with Vinh, Xe, and Quang,[101] the little girls assisting at the clinic. Back then I was their playful and attention-demanding big sister Thuy. Now I am a cadre with heavy responsibilities entrusted to me by the Party.

11 April 1969

With only a few short minutes in the middle of the crowd, I somehow comprehend and feel what those dear eyes are saying to me: We are silent, but we understand each other entirely.

Good-bye, dearest dark eyes.[102]

12 April 1969

What am I waiting for? What am I unsatisfied with? Why do I feel so frustrated? Perhaps there is nothing I want for myself. What else can I ask? Everyone already loves and pampers me. Before my eyes, life is verdant with hope despite the clouds brooding in the corner of the sky.

Are duties making me restless? It's very possible. My tasks are heavy, but there are not enough people—I am afraid I cannot guarantee the quality of my work.

And what else, Thuy? Why is your heart ruled by sorrow and yearning when it is supposed to be totally devoted to the Party?

But . . . the Party does not say a communist's heart knows only reason and work.

---

[101] These young women were on staff at the clinic.

[102] Thuy is probably referring to Thuan, her adopted young brother.

A heart is also capable of love and hope . . . so you cannot blame yourself, Thuy!

16 April 1969

I have another dear friend here in the South. So from now on you're my big brother, aren't you, Tan? I am a little lost when I think that although you're busy with a thousand tasks as district secretary, you still have time for me—a young sister from the North whom you consider kin—you still reserve your thoughts, worries, and longings for me.

It's exactly as Nghi[103] says in a letter I received today from the North: "Our revolution is magical because it opens our hearts and eyes to a beautiful world; there the fire of love is brightly lit, even though today's life is dangerous and painful."

Big brother Tan, you can believe in me, believe in the loyalty and sincerity of your little sister.

17 April 1969

I sit by my young brother. His ragged breathing and his feverish body under the thin blanket fill my heart with sorrow and love. I want to hold him and share his exhaustion. I want to hug him, hold him in my arms like a mother cuddling her sick child. That sentiment is honorable but . . . I cannot act on it because not everyone in this life can understand such honorable love. There are many scrutinizing eyes and detestable rumors.

---

[103]Nghi was a student friend studying in Hanoi.

How sad! When can society rid itself of those outdated thoughts? When will people live entirely by affection, by a pure and clear soul?

Oh, my young brother! Understand my love, feel it in the gentle touch of my hand on your forehead, see it deep in my affectionate eyes, recognize this love that I cannot express to you in words.

22 *April* 1969

A heart-wrenching farewell. There is too much to say, so we say nothing. There is enough time to talk, but I don't have enough words to explain my love to you, to make you understand its full complexity. And I know it's the same for you, sitting here next to me, your eyes dark with sorrow, your voice broken with emotion. "Sister, leaving you this time, I am sadder than ever that my dream to live by your side cannot be realized. This time I don't know how soon I will see you again."

What can I say to that? How can I say anything meaningful when my heart is as heavy as yours with sorrow and anxiety?

The perilous month of May will come to collect the high price in blood and bones for the final victory. If you sacrifice yourself like the other heroes . . . what will I do then, young brother?

You tell me that if you perish, I must think that you are still by my side; I should still see your dear face and hear your faithful, affectionate words.

It is not necessary for you to say that, I already know it. But that will be excruciating.

How can my happiness be complete if you are no longer alive?

No, be with me forever, young brother. Don't go anywhere!

24 April 1969

I've learned from my relationships: "Don't trust people too easily." Affection must be proven by action, not only by words in letters. That's a lesson, Thuy! Life is still full of thorns, full of opportunistic worms competing for a meager reputation, a meager benefit. So don't be surprised. I only need to remind myself to be aware, to be ever vigilant. I've already had two hard realities: M. and Nghia. Aren't they a lesson, Thuy?

Oh, Thuy, you're already twenty-six, twenty-seven years old, but you don't even have the experience of someone half your age.

I must pare away my romantic notions. I must diminish the purity and innocence in my heart. I must be more calculating and more cautious in my actions. I must show wisdom and shrewdness commensurate with my position.

Oh, Thuy! You want to live with a clear vision, a fresh hope, an intense love, and a wholesome life. Yours is an impossible dream.

26 April 1969

Sister Xuyen[104] returns without a shred of good news, bearing only more woes.

I try to keep calm during the conversation, but my heart is crushed. You are still sick, young brother, but dangers loom all around you. I could see sadness coming into your teary eyes, shadowing your thin pale face.

---

[104]Nguyen Thi Kim Xuyen was a member of the clinic staff.

I don't know what I can do to protect my beloved young brother.

27 April 1969

Perhaps nothing is sadder than an evacuation scene, the houses abandoned, gutted of furniture, devoid of life. This afternoon as I return to the clinic[105] from the forest, the enemy is not far away— I look at the lovely houses, and my heart fills with hatred. These houses bear so much of our efforts. So much sweat has permeated each straw stalk and stone. If we must leave this place, when can we have such treatment facilities again? I am not pessimistic, but I feel a strange sadness laced with anxieties.

Last night, a dream of peace came to me in that chaotic, empty house. I dreamed of Hanoi and the large cool rooms with their beige walls at Chu Van An High School; I dreamed of a music book, within its pages a lock of young Thanh Tra's silky golden hair and Hao's chrysanthemum. And I saw Dad, Mom, Uncle Hien, brother Bieu,[106] and all my dear ones in the North.

Oh, the dream is not mine alone, but it's the dream of Peace and Independence burning in the hearts of thirty million Vietnamese and in millions of people around the world.

Tonight all is silent in the deserted forest. The moon shines

---

[105]In a future entry, dated January 15, 1970, Thuy reveals that this clinic was near Dong Ram in Duc Pho District.

[106]Do Kim Hao was Thuy's best friend, and Nguyen Bieu was Hao's husband. In the entry of April 17, 1969, Thuy describes her dream about a silky lock of hair from Hao's daughter Tranh Tra, which Hao had tied to dried chrysanthemums and placed in a book. Tranh Tra was two years old when Thuy left for the South.

faintly, perhaps, sharing the same thought of protecting the silence of the clinic.

Sitting alone on the bench in front of the operating room, looking around . . . I cannot hold off the sadness seeping into my heart. Tomorrow the entire clinic will go into a grand plan of countering the enemy.

28 April 1969

Despite our anticipation, we still have a considerable amount of trouble. This morning, following the decision of the clinic leadership in the meeting last night, we move all seriously injured soldiers and handicapped patients to the Party's school because the enemy can reach the clinic.

It's not yet 8:30 a.m., but I urge people to move the injured. I follow them, carrying as many supplies as possible. We trudge up the slope to the school, sweat pouring down our faces, but we dare not pause to rest. We are so exhausted I have to encourage some to return to the clinic and carry the last three stretchers.

Less than an hour and a half later, a barrage of gunshots goes off nearby, so close to us that it seems the enemy has already reached the guard station. I tell all the patients to prepare for another move. We are not ready to do anything, but our terror-stricken highlander[107] guerrilla brothers rush in, saying that the

---

[107] The collective English term for the indigenous ethnic minorities who live mainly at higher elevations. The French referred to them as *montagnards,* or "mountain people." There are fifty-three ethnic minority groups in Vietnam. In this case, Thuy is writing about someone from the H'Re group.

enemy has reached the irrigation gutter. All the local people are fleeing the area.

The task force assigned to transporting injured soldiers hasn't returned. There are still five stretchers to carry, but I am here with only Tam and a few Phase-1 students[108] who are preparing to return home. "We cannot leave the injured. We must try our best to carry them, comrades!" I say, but I am worried. My comrades are a few skinny, sickly teenagers. The situation is becoming very perilous. Tam and Quang run back in a panic: the enemy has arrived at the stream where we used to bathe.

Several stretchers have been moved. Kiem, a wounded soldier with a broken leg, is on the last stretcher. I don't know what to do, so I call one of the students, Ly[109]—a little girl—to help me carry Kiem. He is big, too heavy for the two of us to lift. We try with all our strength, but we can only drag him out of the house for a short distance. I have to leave him there and go for help. Fortunately, I meet Co and Minh. Between ragged breaths, they say that the enemy has shot Comrade Van, one of the wounded soldiers. Together we go back and carry Kiem down a hole, where we hide from the enemy.

All the injured patients regroup an hour later. Van is the only one missing. Nine of our cadres are also missing.

We decide to move to Ho Sau[110] to take advantage of Unit 120's position[111] and supplies as discussed in our meeting yesterday.

---

[108]With almost everyone involved in the war effort, there was a limited amount of manpower. These men might have been guerrillas from Pho Cuong who helped Thuy at the clinic.

[109]Ly was one of Thuy's medical students. Part of Thuy's responsibilities, besides healing patients and performing operations, was to train medical staff.

[110]Ho Sau was in the vicinity of the clinic, in the same mountainous region of Pho Cuong village.

[111]There were three NLF units based in the delta region of Quang Ngai Province. They were organized by name and region: Pho Vinh, Pho Hiep, and Unit 120.

It's an extremely arduous move. Perhaps it's like the other moves when the clinic was under air raid or attack, but it seems much harder this time because we cannot rely on anyone else. Ill and frail people, who are probably too weak for the hike, must now also carry stretchers. We climb mountains and cross streams to get to the new place.

Exhausted, our legs shaking with hunger, we are still very calm. The perilous years have made us mature in the face of danger.

At 4:00 p.m., we arrive at our destination.

Tonight, moonlight floods the forest. After visiting the injured and finding that we have suffered nothing serious, I lie down to rest. Arm on my forehead, watching the moon, I cannot calm my thoughts.

Two full years have passed. It was under the full April moon when I first came to Duc Pho to take on duties; the clinic had been destroyed by an air raid. Now it's April again. . . . The April sun in the South is blindingly bright. And my hatred burns as hot as that summer sun. This afternoon, when I stood at the top of a tall mountain and saw thick smoke rising from the old clinic, my eyes filled with tears. So much sweat and effort, so much money and so many other resources the people have contributed to the clinic! It's all dust and ashes now!

What can I say, comrades?

I can only repeat our unchanging Vietnamese conviction: "There is no other way than to fight until not one imperialist American remains in our country. Only then we can have happiness."

29 April 1969

At 1:30 a.m., I wake up. The vast forest is quiet in the dim moon-light. The Liberation Radio[112] is playing a *vong co* song.[113] The lyric and rhythm of the song penetrate deeply into my heart.

All at once, I miss home so much.

Is this quiet night forest making me lonely?

Is being in danger and homeless reminding me of the warm room with Dad, Mom, and my happy family?

Oh, Thuy, tonight you are not the only one alone; besides you, forty people including injured comrades, their wounds still raw, share the same fate. And millions of Vietnamese are still engulfed in flames, smoke, and hatred.

Surely you know that, don't you?

2 May 1969

I am not facing these difficulties alone. Around me, comrades and friends all worry about the clinic. In the tide of incoming letters was one extremely touching missive brimming with affection, concern, and immeasurable tenderness. Thank you, everyone! I promise all of you that we—especially I—will calmly overcome all these obstacles, we will stand firmly like victors.

---

[112]Local PRG broadcasting was referred to as "Liberation Radio." Listening to the radio was one of Thuy's pleasures during the war. Music was central to the last days of her life.

[113] *Vong co* is a genre of folksong very popular in South Vietnam, usually sung by a solo male singer accompanied by a guitar or a Vietnamese stringed instrument. The song consists of six lines. The lyric and rhythm require the singer to hold a high note to showcase his virtuosity.

3 May 1969

Returned to Pho Cuong after nearly one year. This dear land that I consider home is unchanged. The people of Pho Cuong, old acquaintances and new ones, all welcome me warmly. But I am unhappy because all my dear ones are absent. I do not see anyone.

The little girl Dang is sick. She is angry with me because I have decided to leave, despite her nagging me to stay an extra day. Her anger makes me sadder. Lying beside her, I could not sleep. My eyes keep turning to the lonely moon shining in the immense sky.

Dear young brother, why aren't you here? You love me, but you do not yearn for me the way I do when I wait for you.

I know I am wrong because I cannot blame anyone. Who can go anywhere while the Americans are still here? Yet I'm frustrated.

Oh, Thuy, you little girl! You are still a child, you let sentiment overcome reason.

11 May 1969

The reconstruction of the clinic has begun. Everyone is focused on that task. Lien, Vinh,[114] brother Sau, sister Xang,[115] and I are the only people staying back with the injured.

The air is hot and heavy on this humid afternoon. The wind cannot penetrate this valley. Enemy planes roar across the broad sky, no pause in the explosions of bombs and artillery shells . . . a

---

[114]Vinh held a staff position at the clinic.

[115]A cook for the clinic, Nguyen Thi Xang was one of the last two staff members who stayed behind with Thuy to tend to the most severely wounded patients prior to the attack by the U.S. military on June 20, 1970.

worrisome feeling presses heavily on my heart. There are only five of us here, but there are six stretchers to move. All our assets are gathered here—the surrounding topography makes retreat very difficult—if the enemies come . . . how can I cope with that?

The victorious day is not far, but how much blood and bone will be littered on that remaining stretch of road, dear comrades? I have never been pessimistic, although I do think that sacrifice is natural for everyone in times like these.

12 May 1969

The conversations with big brother Long[116] have left me with some remarkable thoughts. I knew him under the hardships of the clinic reconstruction. That fair and slender leader looked at me with joyful, smiling eyes and said, "Try, little sister, try to learn and grow in your profession and in leadership." A machete in hand, his pants rolled up, he went to work with me in the rain. Soon afterwards, he went away. Although he lived close to me for only a short time, he still grew to love me very much. The letters he sent back were always filled with affection and concern. Thuan and brother Ky often called him "a rare person." Once Thuan said, "In my life I only love and admire two people for the way they live, brother Long and you, sister." The boy's love placed me too high in his esteem, but he's right about Long.

Sitting and listening to Long talking about his days on duty, I blurted out, "Had I been with you, I would have learned so

---

[116]Nguyen Duc Long was chief of the medical department of Duc Pho District.

many valuable things!" I really wish I could return to work with him. It would have been possible if there were no change in the reorganization.

13 May 1969

I returned to Pho Cuong after fierce fighting there. The air is still heavy with the stench of the battlefield. The army is handling the injured and dead. I don't know why the joy of victory (ninety-eight of the enemy killed, an HU-1A[117] shot down, one tank) does not overcome sadness. Is this happening only to me, or to everyone?

Fifteen comrades sacrificed their lives, twenty-one injured—that's not a small number.

The hamlet is quiet. The enemy's guns sound like popcorn. Unafraid, I feel pensive and hateful.

Sitting by you (we have been yearning for this, haven't we?), somehow the joy is not complete. . . . With only starlight and the enemy's flares, I try to see in the dark what your shiny eyes want to say, but I do not see anything more than your usual look of intense love. And like the other times, you sit quietly beside me, not knowing what to say.

We are alike, never satisfied with anything—duties and

---

[117]Of the five major types of helicopters used during the war, the utility helicopter (UH) played the largest role. Nicknamed "Hueys," these helicopters could transport troops into combat or function as weapon platforms for machine guns or rocket and grenade launchers. In 1970, two-thirds of the 3,900 helicopters in operation in Vietnam were Hueys. Responsible for the deaths of many military and civilian Vietnamese, the Hueys also saved many American lives by airlifting more than 390,000 soldiers to medical facilities. The NLF forces had no aircraft.

sentiments. Nothing is ever enough. Is this our desire to advance or our overreaching ambition?

18 May 1969

The fighting continues, volleys of gunshots reverberating day and night, the roar of planes tearing the air, every night the enemy's flares illuminating a corner of the sky in the direction of the district seat. The fighting grows fiercer by the day. Our soldiers lie day and night in the battlefield, enduring bombs, bullets, and the scorching sun. Oh, liberation brothers, you are the ones who endure the most peril. Your blood flows to soak the flag as well as the land you are protecting. Somehow at this moment, more than ever, I feel deeply that your heroic sacrifices are so noble and divine. The whole South is on the attack. You are everywhere. You are numerous. I know many of you are from the socialist North. Also, many of you joined the fighting after we had peace in the North.[118]

The other day I met some very young scouts, their skin still fair, the hair on their cheeks still soft and downy—probably high school students who recently dropped their pens to take up guns, embarking on the journey to fight the Americans and save the country.

That's it, the whole nation is on the road, the whole nation is throwing itself into battle. We certainly must defeat the American invaders, must bring ourselves to the days of independence and freedom.

---

[118]Thuy is referring to the fact that many of those who were fighting in the South were, like herself, volunteers from the North who chose to leave a somewhat peaceful setting to fight in a dangerous war.

18 May 1969

Why did I treat young brother like that? Certainly, you will be sad. But that's me, I behave in the same way toward everyone. There are times when I cause grief for my dear ones. This is not an effect of my character, but the result of the extreme complexity of my affections. I demand too much of my dear ones. I never demand anything materialistic, but my spiritual demand is very high.

So many times Thuan says that he loves me more than anyone except his parents. Even so, sometimes I still doubt his love. Hearing that the situation in Pho Cuong is tense, and knowing that he is under tremendous hardship, I want to comfort him, but I still send that letter, a letter containing several lines of blame.

Oh, brother, I always love you immensely, but love is not only sunny, rosy mornings, calm afternoons, or moonlit nights on the vast and peaceful rice fields. Love is also the storms after the calm summer days.

So, that's what it is. Befriending a bourgeois is very complicated.

20 May 1969

Close to death once more. This morning several HU–1As[119] and a small scout plane circled very close to Deep Hole.[120] The intensity

---

[119]We believe she meant UH–1A, the American utility helicopter also known as "Huey" (see note 117). By 1969 the Americans used the UH–1B and later versions, not the UH–1A, though the UH–1A was used by the South Vietnamese air forces at that time.

[120]Deep Hole (Ho Sau) was where the clinic was located during part of 1970. It was so called because it was built partially underground.

of their search worried me very much. After a search close to the treetops, they found a patients' ward. The sounds of exploding grenades burst in our ears, fire broke out, and smoke covered the whole house. Everybody rushed down to the shelter—the shelter is very shallow, but there was no other alternative—I think perhaps it will be hard to escape this time.

When the gunship had circled out farther, I ran back to the room for the wounded soldiers, everyone had gone down to the shelter, including immobile patients. The gunship approached again, circling closer. Its occupants showered grenades down around the house. The sounds of rockets exploding on the slope shook the sky.

I turned to brother Minh, a wounded soldier from the clinic and asked, "What do we do now?"

"Sit here, what else?"

I suddenly thought of my dear ones in both parts of the country, and told myself, Death is so simple! We can only wait for bombs and artillery shells to rain down and tear the small forest apart.

After thirty minutes of shooting, the devils went away. I ran back and moved the injured in a hurry. Carrying Kham on my back, I was tired but still happy that there were no casualties from the attack. That is the happiest thing.

The same day, we all moved to a new location.

Oh, the perilous days of this last stage!

24 May 1969

I return to Pho Cuong just as the fighting begins. At 2:00 a.m., the shooting starts. Bombs, bullets, artillery shells, and airplanes create a maelstrom of sounds, the sounds usually heard in war movies.

Hearing gunshots, I am perturbed because we are very close to the battlefield. I have not had time to go anywhere when Thuan comes out despite the planes overhead and anxiously calls me back to the secret chamber.

At night, Thuan and I witness the battle. The enemy counter-attacks with extreme ferocity. Jet planes drop bombs all over the hamlet; an OV-10[121] plane circles above, shining light and firing streams of bullets down onto the battlefield. In the middle of the night, red bullets, like fire, pour down onto the battlefield and into my heart. Who will those bullets hit? Will it be you, the liberation brothers who went with me on the road the other day? Lam, the brothers Den . . . and how many more? I do not sleep the whole night. Worries, anger, and hatred press heavily on my heart.

25 May 1969

The days living by your side have proven your words. Indeed, you treat me differently from anyone else. Your relationship reflects your thoughts and vision about love and desire. These are the important details, the worries, the concerns, the affection, and the pampering you give me. Each word, each look, each drink you bring me, each injection into my arm that you insisted on while I was sick, all prove that you love me more than anyone else. That's all! Is it true, brother?

---

[121]The official name of this plane is the OV-10 Bronco. With its single fuselage positioned between double booms, the OV-10 was initially used by the U.S. Marine Corps for observation squadrons on visual reconnaissance missions, but was also used in armed reconnaissance and helicopter escort, for front-line and low-level photography, and for utility and ground attack.

4 June 1969

The days are still tense. The enemy drops down close to home. They shout, felling trees noisily in the forest. The clinic is quiet, coiled with anticipation.

I am on duty at Pho Cuong. The news leaves me stunned with worry. I am holding a bowl of rice in my hand, but I can no longer eat. Will it be like this forever? We rebuilt the clinic just a few days ago, and now we have to evacuate again—when can we continue our *thu dung*[122] duty? I am peculiarly worried and angry. Is there another way besides running forever without the means to counterattack?

5 June 1969

The enemy has expanded their search. We can no longer stay here. Tonight the majority of cadres and wounded soldiers flee down to Pho Cuong. In the darkness we cannot see each other's faces, but we can feel the pain and sadness of each cadre and patient.

I leave the group to coordinate our duties, and return late at night to find that the wounded have already been fed. They lay scattered in a tangle of bodies and limbs on the veranda of Dang's house, some sleeping, others moaning in pain.

Three non-ambulatory cases remain up there without anyone to transport them. Some lead cadres are with them. I need to return, but it's dangerous to go now. I don't know where the enemy

---

[122]*Thu dung* was the task of readmitting lost cadres and soldiers, deserters, and convalescing personnel who were absent without permission, motivating them, and returning them to their units.

is hiding. But what can I do? Duty demands that I must return, even if it costs me my life.

The night grows late, but no one closes his eyes. Thuan sits quietly by my side, not saying a word. When we are about to leave, he says, "I don't know about you, sister, but I worry so much. . . ."

And I cannot complete my reply: "I leave you the backpack, there is a diary in it. . . ."

I want to say that if I don't come back, he should keep the diary and send it to my family. But I leave the sentence unfinished. In the dim moonlight, we read in each other's eyes the sadness of separation.

He leaves, and some others depart, too. Alone on the veranda of sister Tinh's house, I don't know why tears come to my eyes. Are you crying, Thuy? No, be courageous and persevering in all circumstances. Always keep a smile on your lips despite these thousand perils, Thuy.

11 June 1969

The Provisional Revolutionary Government[123] is formed. It's a historic event, another major step of the revolution. I am delighted in this victory, but I also feel the viciousness of the battlefield more than ever.

---

[123]The Provisional Revolutionary Government (PRG) was established on June 8, 1969, and represented political and military forces in South Vietnam at the Paris Peace Talks. The PRG received diplomatic recognition from communist states. Its foreign minister was Madame Nguyen Thi Binh, who headed the PRG delegation at the Paris Peace Talks. On April 30, 1975, the PRG assumed power as the Republic of South Vietnam for fifteen months until the South and North were officially reunified as the Socialist Republic of Vietnam on July 2, 1976.

All day and night, the sounds of bombs, jet planes, gunships, and HU-1As circling above are deafening. The forest is gouged and scarred by bombs, the remaining trees stained yellow by toxic chemicals.[124] We're affected by the poison, too. All cadres are severely fatigued, their arms and legs weary, their appetites gone. They can neither move nor eat. We want to encourage one another, but there are moments when our worries become clear and undeniable, and the shadow of pessimism creeps upon us.

13 June 1969

I'm going to Pho Cuong. I'm excited and delighted, hoping that this is my opportunity to be with my dear ones for one or two days before starting *thu dung*. But upon my arrival, Thuan tells me of the preparation to receive soldiers of Unit 120 wounded in the attack at the district seat. There are cases of severe injury; Tam is one of them. Hearing the news, I focus my mind entirely on that task.

The wounded are brought in at 10:00 p.m. One of Comrade Loi's organs was fatally punctured.[125] Comrade Thanh's wound is manageable. As for Tam, the boy from Pho Cuong with the very

---

[124]From 1961 to 1971, as part of Operation Ranch Hand, the U.S. military sprayed toxic chemical defoliants over 10 percent of Vietnam. The intention of the herbicidal warfare was to kill vegetation and deny the enemy "cover." The spray contained dioxin, contaminated with TCDD, the most poisonous and durable chemical associated with cancers, birth defects, and other diseases. Because the chemical was stored in fifty-five-gallon drums with large orange stripes, it was given the nickname "Agent Orange."

[125]Thuy Tram did not specify which organ was pierced; it could have been the liver, pancreas, or one of the kidneys.

beautiful voice, big eyes, and lovely character, his leg has been blown off by a mine. He lies still—a serious sign. I am intent on the rescue, my heart heavy with sympathy. It's not that much blood and bones, isn't it? There will be more and much more. Beware, young brother! I talk to him with apprehension. Nobody sleeps through the whole long night. Fatigue and empathy have drained me.

Departure, 3:00 a.m. Young brother escorts me to Ai Pass. Oh, my young brother, don't let anything happen to you.

16 June 1969

The unforgettable memories—unforgettable, but what will I think when I remember them? Sadness? Joy? Regret? Or what, Thuy? You, the girl who knows how to act properly in all circumstances!

17 June 1969

It's not just affection! Affection cannot have this hot intensity; it cannot entirely control a person's emotions. So what can I say? I have always known how to force my heart to follow my mind, so I haven't committed the common mistakes of others. But there is one thing here that surprises me and makes it difficult for me to think clearly. I can neither confirm nor deny that it is a mistake.

So, what now?

Oh! Life is so complicated, and this atrocious war is making it a million times more so.

The sky is still bright tonight. Is it because of the lightning or the flaming flares, or is it because of a pair of black eyes shining bright with love?

Is it the humid heat of summer or the heat of love that's suffocating me?

I feel a mixture of sadness and joy.

No, not joy, there is only sadness weighing heavily on my heart, a heart thirsting for love, but knowing clearly that it can only live with a certain kind of love. That heart can only accept a clean and pure love. Without that, the heart will die. But it's better to die and keep one's honor, one's nobility as a communist.

18 June 1969

Received letters from home, letters imbued with the hue of peace. The roads are bright red with flame trees, and the small room is redolent with the scent of lotus. The familiar radio playing in the middle of the house. Oh! That scene is so far away, my dear siblings. Your sister Thuy only knows the streams of red bullets illuminating the night sky, the bitter tang of artillery shells, the distressing farewells . . . so I feel sad reading your letters.

This time, many people leave for the North, departing with joy and excitement. But when they come to say good-bye, it seems they dare not express their happiness. As for me, I smile brightly to send them off, though afterward I stand still for a long time, unable to say a word.

Oh, Thuy, don't be sad. Promise yourself that when our nation is independent, you also will return to the North. Your joy will certainly be whole then.

25 June 1969

The enemies begin their sweep very early this morning. I just wake up and crawl underground, no time to eat. It has been more than a year and a half since I have had to hide in a secret chamber.[126] The heat in the earth is exhausting, stifling. The situation is very precarious. Enemy forces have spread all over the three hamlets of the village, American soldiers, traitors,[127] and field combat police. My shelter is not far from the enemy. There are four people here, but we haven't closed the trapdoor because of the heat.

At noon, Tan[128] seems tired of standing guard. He sits down next to me and describes the enemy's operation evolving above. Suddenly a traitor cries out. Tan takes a peek and fearfully shuts the trapdoor. The traitor comes within five meters of our hiding place. In the rush, the trapdoor hasn't been closed properly, there are gaps. I hear the enemies' footsteps, scraping over the brushes of wild pineapples, and their calls to each other. Young brother murmured into my ear:

"What if we must sacrifice our lives?"

"Then that's it, what else!"

"No, I won't accept that. It's fine for me, but not for you. What will your parents think . . ."

. . . [illegible] looking at me, eyes seared with immense con-

---

[126]Civilians and military forces fighting the U.S. and Republic of Vietnam (ARVN) soldiers built underground structures to protect themselves. There were three major types. Secret chambers were reserved for important officials or civilian physicians such as Thuy.

[127]By "traitors," Thuy means U.S.-backed South Vietnamese soldiers (ARVN) who fought for the Republic of Vietnam, as well as civilians who worked for the U.S. military or ARVN forces.

[128]Nguyen Tan died some time later. He appeared in some photos with the late Nguyen van Gia, war reporter, taken at Nga Man.

cern. I turn away, not daring to look in there any longer. In those eyes are the words Kho-riu-chi-a said to Pavel[129] in jail. My heart is stirred by a deep sorrow; I am sorry for my young brother and for myself. But there is no other way. I am doing just as Pavel would have done in this circumstance.

This war is so perilous. I wish you, Thuy, would stand firm in the stance of a communist.

Giau's[130] death caught me off guard. In the sweeping operation today, spies pointed out Giau's underground shelter, several claymore mines. Sprays of bullets killed Giau and five other guerrillas.

Only the other night, I met Giau at Xuan Thanh.[131] The senior nurse of Pho Cuong was happy to see me again. He was very different from the previous times I'd seen him. It seemed that among the tasks Thuan transferred to Giau, there was one that was understood without being mentioned—the responsibility of protecting me, a cadre from the district and Thuan's dear friend. Giau accepted this charge completely. In Thuan's place, Giau took me to work, from one place to the next. When the night was late, he took me back to Thuan's house and asked Thuan softly, "Now shall we let sister Tram stay here with you or at my place?" My brother answered, "It's up to you." Giau left me with Thuan and said to him, "Please take care of sister Thuy Tram, brother." He did not leave until very late at night.

---

[129]Kho-riu-chi-a is Thuy's phonetic spelling for a character in the novel *How the Steel Was Tempered,* by Nikolai Ostrovsky (see note 1).

[130]Giau was a medic and part of the leadership of Pho Cuon village. He was killed on June 16, 1969.

[131]Xuan Thanh is a hamlet in Pho Cuong village.

I could not have imagined that night walking with him around the hamlet, eating cucumbers with him, and sharing the late-night rice soup with his warm family would be the last time I spent with him.

Tonight it is the same moonlight, the same people, the same scene, but he is already laid immobile beneath three feet of earth.

Holding the little baby in her arms, his wife sits unmoving, like a cadaver. I don't know what to say to her. My eyes brim with tears when she says, her words choking with grief, "He is dead, but you, Second Sister, and Third Brother must avoid being lost."[132]

Oh, what to say besides the word *revenge*. Revenge for the fallen and for us, the living who suffer in this well of anger and pain.

Young brother looks at me one more time, his two black eyes talking to me in silence: *Life is so short, isn't it, sister? What shall we do so we won't regret when we die?*

29 June 1969

There are deaths that tear the hearts of the living. One case of leg amputation caused by a mine has arrived at the clinic at 3:15 a.m. It's Lien, a comrade from the Pho Cuong village unit. Just the other day he led me to a hidden shelter. Today, looking at him, my heart burns with worries: What if my dear ones meet a similar fate? Then that's it, what else?

---

[132]The woman addressed Thuy as her oldest sibling and Thuan as her second sibling out of courtesy or respect.

July 1969

This afternoon I leave Pho Cuong temporarily to go to work at the North Wing.[133] On the way, I pass the strategic line and walk into the deadly segment of road called Khe Sanh.[134]

Leaving this dear familiar land, my heart stirs with yearnings. This poor land has bonded so deeply with me. From all the mothers, the sisters, the local cadres, to the guerrillas, I know almost everyone and I am well liked. Everywhere I walk in this hamlet, the familiar greeting "Second Sister" welcomes me, many hands reaching out for mine, these fine intimate touches.

And . . . there is nothing comparable to the intense affection my young brother reserved only for me. He sat there, head bent on the table, worried to see me walk into danger. His hands seized mine. I felt his hands shaking with love and fear. Eyes heavy with sadness, he asked me, "Sister, will you return to me?"

I wanted to encourage him, so I did not disclose the thought that troubled me: Would I be able to run as I passed through Khe Sanh? I still smiled to him cheerfully, despite the sorrow in my heart. Perhaps this was the last time we would see each other. Oh, young brother, how can I capture your whole image to keep with me in the perilous coming days? How can I have such a brother who loves me so much?

---

[133]Thuy is referring to going to the north side of Duc Pho.

[134]Khe Sanh was the section of road from Pho Vinh to Pho Minh. American forces blanketed the entire area with electronic equipment to detect movements of the revolutionary fighters and supporters in this area of Quang Ngai Province. One of the most dangerous roads in the central region during the war, it is not to be confused with the Khe Sanh that appears on most maps as the capital of Quang Tri Province, nor is it the U.S. combat base of that name that was the site of a famous battle in 1968.

Okay, good-bye all, I promise to see you again with joy. The day of our reunion is not far away.

8 July 1969

I return to the familiar house with the *O-ma* tree[135] by the well, and see Nghia, Thuong, and this homeland Pho Hiep again.

One afternoon talking with Nghia isn't enough to break down all the barriers of our distant relationship as sister and brother. In any case, I want "the sky to be blue again after the storm." I forgive him for all his mistakes, and my heart lightens a little when I see him reverting to our old connection, full of affection.

Tonight, as I pass through Khe Sanh,[136] everybody is worried for me. . . . Cho takes me close to Vinh Phuoc—This little sister's concern for my welfare is very moving. I haven't fully seen her kindness until now. At first I thought that Thuan's anxieties affected her, but now I see that her feelings are her own and genuine. From crossing the strategic line over the lake to getting a meal, Cho has taken care of everything for me, from a bowl of rice to a piece of fish.

Once in a while she sighs and says, "Sister, you will pass through Khe Sanh, where bombs and bullets fall like rain. How can I leave you alone? Perhaps I should walk with you through Khe Sanh, then return on my own?"

---

[135] *O-ma* is a tropical shrub with a sweet, fat fruit.

[136] See note 134.

I caress her hair and smile. "It's not a problem, I can pass. And if bad luck happens, then that is something no one can prevent!"

But in the darkest part of the night, I walk through Khe Sanh without an artillery shell, a flare, or a tirade of guns. It seems the enemy has sympathy for a weak girl who is used to being loved and pampered since childhood.

12 July 1969

In these leisurely days, I have so much time to think.

What thoughts lower the shadow of sadness over your eyes, Thuy?

Of course, yearnings unsettle my heart.

Oh, the dear South Wing! Over there, certainly, my dear ones still worry for me and miss me; a pair of dark eyes is losing sleep in the long nights ruptured by the continuous explosions of bombs at the north side.

Standing here, I strain to look across the mountains toward the South Wing and to recognize the eroded part of the mountain at Pho Cuong. Immense longings!

Going away, I leave at home a thousand difficulties. Trung is probably dead, and the comrade with a gangrened arm may not survive. . . . The brothers and sisters at home certainly suffer many hardships. I empathize deeply with the brothers and sisters, the Tus, the Kys, the Lanhs, the Liens. . . .

My young brother's strange love makes me unhappy; that love rarely brings pure and shining joy, but rather worry and sadness. It seems the thing I once thought untouchable has been harmed. What will life be like?

14 July 1969

Today is Dad's birthday, I remember, despite all the bombs and bullets; just yesterday, artillery salvos killed five people and wounded two. I was also in the impact zone of those extremely heavy rounds. Everybody still hasn't recovered from fear and shock. Nevertheless, I am still the same as always, my heart heavy with longings, worries, and thoughts.

Beloved Dad, Mom, and sisters out there, you cannot see life here in its entirety. It's a life of extreme heroism, extreme perils where death and sacrifices come easier than eating a meal. Nevertheless, people still fight with determination. I am one of those hundreds of thousands. I live to fight, and I have the feeling that one day I will fall for the future of our people. I will not be there when they sing the victory song. I am proud to offer my entire life to the country.

Of course, I would also grieve for not having a part in the peaceful life that everyone, including myself, has sacrificed blood and bones to secure. But that's nothing; millions of people have already fallen, but they never had a day of happiness. Therefore, there is no regret!

This afternoon I feel an immense sadness again, strangely longing for my young brother. What are you doing now? I imagine you lying in your hammock, eyes immensely sad. Longing makes your face thin and hollow. Oh, what can I say to you now, strange young brother?

16 July 1969

I don't know what people think when they see the American bandits' air raids. This afternoon, like other afternoons, an OV-10 plane circles several times above the hamlets, then launches a rocket down to Hamlet 13 in Pho An.[137] Immediately, two jets take turn diving down. Where each bomb strikes, fire and smoke flare up; the napalm bomb flashes, then explodes in a red ball of fire, leaving dark, thick smoke that climbs into the sky. Still, the airplanes scream overhead, a series of bombs raining down with each pass, the explosions deafening.[138]

From a position nearby, I sit with silent fury in my heart. Who is burned in that fire and smoke? In those heaven-shaking explosions, whose bodies are annihilated in the bomb craters? The old lady sitting by me stares at the hamlet and says, "That's where Hung's mother-in-law lives."

Oh, my heroic people, perhaps no one on earth has suffered more than you, citizens of this courageous South.

20 July 1969

The class for obstetricians in the Zone is over. Among those leaving to work far away is Second Sister, assigned to Gia Lai. She sends back a letter with scratchy lines full of tears. I empathize

---

[137]Hamlet 13 was part of Pho An village.

[138]Aside from the destruction of the bombs, the noise and vibrations were frightening and deafening. At times, PRG and North Vietnamese troops would also wear protective ear covering.

with her immensely; one only goes away to a place like that to answer the Party's call of duty. I remember when I stepped on the car taking me to the South, I also cried tears of longing, pain, and pride. But she goes away with only pain, tears rolling down her sad face. She brushes them away. She must go because she is a Party member.

The departures continue. I know so many people departing because of duties. I am not sure they have enough pride and enthusiasm as they step onto the road to victory. Why is that? It's easy to understand: the battlefield demands are too high, and those in the rear have already given all to the front for many years.

What does that mean, Thuy?

Does it mean you have a shade of pessimism in you?

22 July 1969

A rainy afternoon away from home.

My sadness and longing are as thick and heavy as the screen of rain shrouding the sky. I find myself very much to blame for inappropriate behavior: in the midst of fiery attacks, I allow my heart to falter. In fact, it is not because of the rain, not because the thatched house is not enough to shield me from the weather. I feel sad in this lonely deserted house. Since coming down to live in the lowlands[139] several days ago, I feel oddly melancholic.

The morning sun rising over the sea, the sun setting on the far

---

[139]Major rivers divide into small rivulets, feeding water into flat, open areas. When Thuy refers to the coastal lowlands or delta, she is referring to flatlands (where rice was grown if the fighting allowed) between the mountains and the coastline. The central provinces, such as Quang Ngai, are the narrowest part of the country, where the mountains are relatively close to the sea.

fields and the bright moonlit nights on the sandy beaches . . . all are beautiful scenes, but I do not find joy. What joy can there be when daily sufferings and death still weigh heavily on our lives? Just yesterday, in a mopping-up operation, the enemy killed five people. Every afternoon they bomb the hamlets.

What joy can there be when our people are scattered and our longings never end? The letters sent to me are short and distressing; my dear ones remind me to be careful. They worry for me each minute, each second. Oh, what to say now. . . .

This afternoon I receive Young Brother's letter informing me of his preparations to go work in Zone 6. Hearing the news, I grieve as though it were a tragedy. If you go . . . I lose my firmest support in this land. That's the truth because no one loves me, cares for me, and understands me as you do. Even M. does not love me the way you do. It's strange because there is no ardent love like yours, even though ours is only a love between a sister and a brother, a revolutionist's love. . . .

23 July 1969

Brother Dao hands me an American cigarette lighter engraved with my name and the name of my beloved comrade. He asks me who did the engraving. I laugh innocently, then return it to him, but on the way home, my heart stirs.

Oh, M.! Why did you engrave my name next to yours? Was it because of the old romantic days? Was it because you still love me passionately, or was it simply some ordinary thing you do?

In fact, few people act without thinking. M. certainly is not like that. But M., tell me why you engraved my name next to yours—the name of a liberation soldier who you often say is no match for a medical student?

24 July 1969

I see San again in the lowlands. He does not expect to meet me. He stands still, speechless with joy and surprise. He is preparing to go to the North, so he insists I visit his place.

Obliging him, I walk with San across the flooded fields of Pho Van, under a mighty downpour. The two of us seek shelter at his acquaintance's house, but the Americans have recently burned it. A single sheet of corrugated metal is all that is left of the roof, not enough to cover the seating space for our host and us. I feel their inconvenience and urge San to leave.

Our hostess says sadly, "Why don't you stay for the meal? Are you afraid the rice is not cooked?"

Indeed, San and I don't want to stay for the meal. Certainly the pot of rice can't be cooked over the feeble fire, which grows faint before our eyes until only the few twigs in the center are burning. The pot goes from a boil to a simmer, then to stillness. The fire is dying, and rain is dripping into the pot.

Are movie directors out there filming a scene like this?

A simple scene, but it says a great deal about the crimes of war.

Among the guests dodging the rain is a comrade who laughs as he regales us with a story about the old days when the enemy first started to create havoc. In those days the hamlet was populous and wealthy, only a few houses were burned. At Tet, one homeowner made offerings to his ancestors on a burned door used as an altar in the middle of his burned house. The comrade and neighbors came to visit. Looking at the scene, they were speechless. They couldn't say a word to motivate the victim.

Now it's the same for houses all over the hamlet, and this afternoon the comrade laughs at the scene before us! We are not defeated; the enemies have burned this house, but we will build another. It's not hard, a few palm leaves are enough. Life in war has minimal requirements. Life is only fighting and working. For personal sustenance: a pot of rice with pickled fish, a sheet of plastic to spread out in an artillery shelter, clothes, rice, and salt in a pair of baskets ready to be borne away on our shoulders when the enemy comes.

Oh, San, when you arrive in the North, remember to tell people who are living in the land of socialism that the South is still suffering, that there is real life only when the American bandits are no longer here.

26 July 1969

Last night the team of guerrillas carrying ammunition through Khe Sanh was ambushed by Americans at Portal Mountain. The American ambush team was sleeping like the dead, scattered haphazardly on the rocks. Our comrades only noticed them at very close range. In the rush, one comrade slipped and fell down a chasm. Fortunately, a rock ledge saved his fall. The Americans threw grenades, but our side suffered no casualties. At 1:00 a.m., the team arrived at Pho An. Looking for Hung (leader of the hamlet unit) to arrange for places to sleep, they told their story.

Lying in the shelter, I listened to the story but didn't come out so I didn't know that Nhieu—Thuan's youngest brother—was in the group.

In the morning, learning that a Nga Man[140] guerrilla is in the group, I knew instantly that it must be Nhieu, an innocent young brother with whom I have a deep bond. I rush to look for him, but the enemy is coming. People have already led him to another hiding place. I'm very disappointed because I want to see him, this little brother, to hold his hand, to console and motivate him with the love of a big sister. And, oh, little brother, your image is the image of the young brother that I've missed day and night.

The road before you is still full of thorns and hardships. I wish you strength and stability on your journey.

27 July 1969

The enemy attacks the hamlet at 6:30 p.m.—in every house, people are having dinner. Folks stop their meals, shoulder their belongings, and evacuate in a hurry. I don't follow them. I plan to go down to the shelter if something happens. I continue to eat as bullets whistle overhead.

It's dark before Tam and Hung come home. Evaluating the situation, we find that it's not possible to stay, so we decide to scatter. I go to Pho Quang, while Tam and Hung run to 18; Chin is too slow, so I don't wait.

I feel deplorable, going alone at dusk down the middle of the deserted hamlet. There is not a soul around. I arrive at Phuong's house. Without people, the house is eerily empty with all the trees

---

[140]Nga Man is a hamlet in Pho Cuong village.

felled by the shelling and the rancid smell of gunpowder lingering in the air, the courtyard and the road full of artillery craters. I run to sister Thinh's house. She says everyone has fled out to the hills, but we cannot follow them at the moment because of the shelling. Indeed, she is talking when artillery shells explode nearby. Fire illuminates our entire area. I resign myself to stay at Thinh's house.

Tonight is the first night I have to be alone without someone to protect me besides these civilians.[141] In nearly two years, wherever I went I always felt untroubled. Despite tense situations, I felt safe because there were people to protect me. Relying on them, I did not have to worry. Tonight I am alone. The first time in the South I must think: If the enemy comes, where should I run? If they attack tonight, what should I decide? Whom do I need to contact for shelter?

The artillery shelter is narrow and hot, so my host and I lie down on the veranda. Either the mosquitoes are pestering me or my mind is restless; I cannot sleep. It's late, the radio has played its last broadcast, but I'm not asleep.

In the hamlet, a dog barks. I sit up, staring into the night trying to guess the situation. Suddenly an unreasonable and intense wish rises in me. I wish to see a dear one on that road, I wish to see you, young brother. You will meet me at this moment. Perhaps I will put my face in your hardened arms, my tears will wet your hands, but I will not explain why.

Why can't I think of someone else other than you, young brother?

---

[141] Twice in her diary, Thuy mentions being protected. Physicians were a precious commodity during the war. However, physicians and nurses were given no privileged treatment. They were expected to work as part of their team, whether in the fields or carrying their own allotment of rice.

It's easy to understand; in all the perils of this southern land, you are there to care for me, to protect me in each little matter, to love and pamper me. I haven't had to do a single thing; you would not let me do even a small task. You would not let me walk alone even for a short distance. . . .

What are you doing now?

Do you know that tonight I am alone, lost and unprotected, in this evasive maneuver?

29 July 1969

The war is extremely cruel. This morning, they bring me a wounded soldier. A phosphorus bomb[142] has burned his entire body. An hour after being hit, he is still burning, smoke rising from his body. This is Khanh, a twenty-year-old man, the son of a sister cadre in the hamlet where I'm staying. An unfortunate accident caused the bomb to explode and severely burned the man. Nobody recognizes him as the cheerful, handsome man he once was. Today his smiling, joyful black eyes have been reduced to two little holes—the yellowish eyelids are cooked. The reeking burn of phosphorus smoke still rises from his body. He looks as if he has been roasted in an oven.

I stand frozen before this heartbreaking tableau.

His mother weeps. Her trembling hands touch her son's body; pieces of his skin fall off, curled up like crumbling sheets of rice cracker. His younger and older sisters are attending him, their eyes full of tears.

---

[142]Phosphorus rounds were fired by artillery as "markers" to locate targets. Although lethal, they were not designed to be used as lethal weapons. When a target was marked with phosphorus, it might then be bombed with napalm. It is not clear whether the young man was hit with a phosphorus round or burned as the result of an accident.

A girl sits by his side, her gentle eyes glassy with worry. Clumps of hair wet with sweat cling to her cheeks, reddened by exhaustion and sorrow. Tu (that's her name) is Khanh's lover.

She carried Khanh here. Hearing that he needed serum for a transfusion, Tu crossed the river to buy it. The river was rising, and Tu didn't know how to swim, but she braved the crossing. Love gave her strength.

The pain is imprinted on the innocent forehead of that beautiful girl. Looking at her, I want to write a poem about the crimes of war, the crimes that have strangled to death millions of pure and bright loves, strangled to death the happiness of millions of people, but I cannot write it.

My pen cannot describe all, even though this is one case I feel with all my senses and emotions.

30 July 1969

At midnight, brother Ky arrives from the South Wing and gives me painful news: the enemy has mounted a surprise attack on the clinic. Young sister Lien was shot and killed while leading the injured to escape. Ky doesn't know who survived among the wounded soldiers and who died. . . .

Within three months, the clinic was attacked four times. My heart burns with worry. Oh, my comrades, who among you survives and who is lost? Who is wandering somewhere? Difficulties are piling on top of our hearts like a big mountain. Do we still have the strength to overturn this immensity, comrades? We must turn it over, otherwise it will crush us to death. There is no other way.

Oh, Lien, the other day when you said good-bye to me, you

reminded me to be careful. But today it is you who have fallen first, the pretty girl who was always excellent in her work. That pampered girl of the clinic no longer exists.

Oh, Lien, for every day that I'm alive, I vow to avenge you and Ly and the millions of people who have fallen in this life-and-death struggle.

31 July 1969

Sister Hanh comes to tell me the real status of the clinic. Three months ago, on the twenty-eighth day, the enemy attacked the clinic for the first time. Now they have just attacked again, on exactly the same day of the month. Lien and brother Tu sacrificed their lives. Tu died on the top of the hill and Le was captured alive.

I am stunned with sorrow, compassion, and fury. I have known that it could happen, but I still cannot stay calm.

Oh, comrades, both dead and alive, we are still together, standing elbow to elbow, side by side, to fight the enemy. You are all still here, Lien, brother Tu, Ly, Huong. There are millions of dear souls standing beside me to live and fight until the day of total victory.

3 August 1969

I see brother Tan after three perilous months engulfed in smoke and fire. For me, Tan is not the district secretary of the Party, but only a dear big brother. I don't know if he would agree that in our relationship I maintain the true nature of a girl grown up in socialism, always maintaining cordial equality and understanding, regardless of our positions.

The day he leaves for the South Wing, I have just arrived from Binh My. I am anxious to see him before his departure. I come at dusk to see him just leaving the house. In the fading light, the hue of his shirt blends with the surroundings. I see his bright smile and shiny dark eyes.

Abruptly I feel a rush of affection for this brother who always possesses a strange optimism. I want to run to him, to put my head on his shoulder the way I did whenever I came home to see Dad or Uncle Hien, but I stand still without uttering a word. There are too many people around me. He shakes my hand, then, after walking away for a distance, he calls back, "Beware, Comrade Tram!" (I understand why he uses the word "comrade.")

Without thinking, I say, "When you arrive there, write back, brother Tan."

I regret saying it; what would people think of that? Does anyone really understand the brother-sister bond we share? Perhaps they're not pleased to see a cadre behaving inappropriately toward a secretary of the Party.

Oh, big brother Tan, this is precisely the thing that worried me when I was considering whether to accept you as my dear big brother. You are a high-level cadre, but I don't want that. If you were merely a cadre of my equal rank, I would be more at ease in our daily interaction as siblings.

What do you think about this, Thuy, young sister of the North, Fifth Brother?[143]

---

[143]In calling Nguyen Trong Tan "Fifth Brother," Thuy indicates that she knows that he is the fourth child of his father. She used this mode of address as a way to show intimacy (only people who know the family well have this information) and respect (because she doesn't call him by his first name).

5 August 1969

I'm on a night emergency-aid mission, going through many dangerous parts of the national highway on which enemy vehicles frequently commute, and passing through the hills filled with American
posts. Lights from the bases shine brightly; I go through the middle
of the fields of Pho Thuan. Bright lights shine from three directions
around me: Chop Mountain, Cactus Mountain, and the flares hang-
ing in midair in front of me. The light sources cast my shadows in
different directions, and I feel like an actor on stage, as in the days
when I was still a medical student performing in a choir. Now I am
also an actor on the stage of life; I am taking the role of a girl in the
liberated area, wearing black pajamas, who, night after night, follows
the guerrillas to work between our areas and those of the enemy.

Perhaps I will meet the enemy, and perhaps I will fall, but I
hold my medical bag firmly regardless, and people will feel sorry
for this girl who was sacrificed for the revolution when she was still
young and full of verdant dreams.

6 August 1969

Sunset on the rice fields always holds a certain poetic sway, regardless of the day's horrors.

Just this morning, the enemy invaded Kim Giao.[144] During the
fighting, two comrades were seriously wounded, and one sacrificed his life.

Deaths still press heavily on me, but this late afternoon, standing

---

[144]Kim Giao is a hamlet in Pho Quang Village.

here in the middle of the golden rice fields, in the glow of the late afternoon, I feel that life still gushes forth. People are still busy with the harvest, and the smile was still bright on the face of the young cadre who walked with me. He is Cong, Lien's lover.[145] Lien died less than ten days ago. Cong grieved long and deeply. But now, in front of me, he smiles brightly, and his conversation is very engaging. Just a while ago, before our departure, he played a cheerful song on the mandolin.

I look at him, feeling strange. What would I be like if I were in his place? Certainly I could not have that smile and that buoyant music.

Oh, how strange is the revolution in this land, with suffering and death unequaled anywhere, but with optimistic eagerness unequaled anywhere.

15 August 1969

Who has ever won without ever having lost?
Who has ever grown wise without ever having been gullible a few times?[146]

One must read and understand To Huu's profound words to keep oneself from becoming pessimistic in moments such as this: In one deployment, two comrades are seriously wounded, six have sacrificed their lives, and ten are captured alive.

Among the dead is brother Dao, the district unit leader of Duc

---

[145]Cong was the boyfriend of Nguyen Thi My Lien.

[146]From the song "Day Ma Di" ("Rise to Go") by Ton That Lap.

Pho. I met him on the first day arriving at Duc Pho; he did not talk much but he was insightful, very close to people, close to the tasks, and he had much public prestige. In this battle he led a squad himself to penetrate deep into the heart of the district seat. A bullet went through his lung from the bottom to the top; the open wound had not been bandaged, so he could not recover.

He was still conscious and in agony. He did not want to bother others. While I tried to resuscitate him, tears ran profusely down my face. I felt immensely sorry for him; I wanted to find every way to save him, but it was impossible. I felt like a soldier with both arms seriously wounded, resigned to see the enemy approaching with gun in hand to kill me—my hands shaking with anger and hatred.

No, I won't surrender. The will to revenge shall give me more strength.

Oh, Dao, do you hear my voice, the voice of your comrade, a young sister, a friend, who vows to avenge you and other comrades who have fallen for our victorious future?

17 August 1969

Receiving your letter, I am a little sad to see you ask, "Does big sister still remember this simple little brother?"

Oh, why are you so naïve, my courageous and intelligent little brother? I always reserve for you my complete affection; I love you and thank you for the noble and unique love you give me. Do you know that this evening, like so many other evenings, I look toward your place? Through the evening fog, I can still recognize the green mountain with a track of red earth, the mountain of your homeland; there, you are missing me and worrying for me, day and night.

How can I ever forget you?

25 August 1969

These are harrowing days. Every night the Americans stalk around the hamlet, hide in the rice fields, and then attack at predawn. This morning they surround the hamlet at first light.

I go down to the shelter, well prepared. Lying in the shelter, listening to their shouting and their search above, I feel the full crush of rage and hate pressing down on me.

Sister Thu Huong, who is the village nurse, and her son were wounded in the raid this morning. I used to stay with her. Just last night we sat together and confided our stories and woes until late. It was the first time I'd heard a woman who had borne a child out of wedlock confess her pains and mistakes. Her chubby baby, as cute as a European toddler, has two pieces of shrapnel in his lung, near the heart.

I don't know if he will survive.[147]

This is war; it spares no one, not a baby or an old woman, and the most hideous thing about it is the bloodthirsty Americans.

29 August 1969

She is a very young mother. Looking at her full face, fair skin, and slim body, few would guess she has a grown son who already

---

[147]This child survived. His name is Tuan, and he lives in Pho Hiep.

served three years in the army. I don't know much about her. Her son, Thien, lives near me. I'm not sure why she shares her feelings about her son with me tonight.

Thien is eighteen this year. His father regrouped to the North, leaving his young wife to raise their son alone. Thien grew up in the miraculous love of his mother. Loving her son too much, she pampered him. Every day, Thien demanded money and cake before going to school, and when he came home, he demanded cake again. If a meal didn't have fish, he became angry and went to school without eating. She often ran after him and begged him to eat so he wouldn't go hungry. At fifteen he demanded to join the army. She didn't give him permission, but he was headstrong. He falsely added one year to his age, then followed a soldier to his unit. She saw her son leave, but she believed that the boy would be back within a week. How could a teenage boy who snacked all day and had never done a single chore since childhood be a soldier? But she was wrong. Thien was attracted to the hard but glorious life. The boy endured many hardships, more than he had ever imagined. Thien grew up. He became a Party member at seventeen. I don't know why he never wrote his mother during the entire three years.

Three years . . . Certainly, Thien cannot comprehend the depth of his mother's love. Three years apart from her son have also been three perilous years at home. In one raid, the enemies destroyed the shelter, the family's last home, with a mine. In the middle of the torrential monsoon, she took her old mother from one place to another, looking for refuge. Sleeping in a corner of someone's veranda during the rainy days, she didn't think much about herself, but instead worried for her son. Where was he? Did he have enough warm clothes? When Thien did not return at the end of the cold season, she fretted that the sweater she'd knitted for him had become too tight for the next season, so she sold it and made a larger one to wait for her son's return. Day and night she searched for news of her son. "Brother, Comrade, do you know Thien at the zone of Operation I?" People looked at her with sympathy, but found her question comically naïve. Oh, heaven, the army is huge, the liberated area is large; how can she ever find him with a question like that?

One day she heard her son was at Unit 48. She ran to the cadre in charge and asked to see her son. He understood her heart and promised to take her to Thien. But after so many days of hard work and the stress of searching for her son, she was exhausted and fell ill for half a month. When she recovered, her son's unit had already left for the front. Again, her suffering life was filled with worry for her son. Once she met an acquaintance from her hamlet. He was on assignment in the same unit with Thien. Learning this bit of news made her happier than if she had won money. She seized the cadre's arm and asked about her son. Hesitantly, he told her that after thrice being denied permission to visit his mother, Thien had gone away somewhere a month ago.

Hearing the news, she became like an insane person. So much longing, hope, and waiting turned into desperation. No longer clearheaded, she cursed that cadre without deliberation: "You do not deserve to be a neighbor because you don't have a shred of compassion for folks of your own homeland. You do not deserve to be a leader because you don't have a sense of camaraderie. . . . You don't understand anything. My son had just left my care, but you have the heart not to let him see his mother after three years apart. Where is my son? If he died on the way to look for me, then . . . do you know what? I will spread the news so no other mother will let her son join the revolution."

She abandoned her tasks and went to Saigon. She didn't have a purpose for the trip, but she knew that if she stayed at home, she certainly would become insane.

Actually, Thien had not abandoned his unit, but had been transferred to a more specialized one. On one of his rice-transport assignments, he'd stopped by his home to visit, but his mother was not home, and he'd left again.

In Saigon, upon hearing the news of her son's return, she bought a ticket to return to Quang Ngai that same afternoon. And when she met her son, she held him in her arms and caressed every strand of hair on his head, every scar on his body. Her son, the soft and spoiled Thien of the old days, had become a strong soldier, tanned and lean. Thien had become a true Party member, a skilled scout seasoned by peril. Her tears fell on her son's green shirt, faded and frayed by many journeys.

Thien requested permission from his unit to stay home for ten days. How can ten days be enough for his mother? It was like a pail of water for a parched summer field. It is nothing. She did not let him return to his unit.

Lying in the hammock strung between two bamboo posts, I listen to her story. I laugh, but tears also fall on the strands of hair draped across my face. I feel for her. I completely understand a mother's love, but there should be a proper resolution so that she can become a symbol of a Vietnamese mother's love. She must know how to love her son and how to offer him to the nation. Oh, sister, do not let that love lead you astray. I will wait for the ending of her story to write it down in my diary.

The night is late, Thien is already soundly asleep, the young soldier once more becoming a child in his mother's loving arms. Oh, Thien, you, the liberation soldier who have struggled on the battlefield with glorious victories, tell me you deserve to be a liberation soldier.

30 August 1969

I have been strangely restless in the last few days. Fierce fighting at Pho Cuong makes me very anxious. Day and night, I feel unsettled. My intuition warns me of something unfortunate. . . . Indeed, this afternoon, sad news came with news of victory from the South Wing.

In one night of continuous fighting, we destroyed fourteen tanks, one HU–1A and fifteen army trucks, and killed 150 Americans. One guerrilla sacrificed his life, and two comrades were wounded. Oh, why must that guerrilla be the orphan Nhieu, Thuan's beloved young brother? The more I am sorry for Nhieu, the more I feel sorry for Thuan. Surely his heart is withering with this loss. Oh, young brother, I understand your heart, the heart of an orphan struggling to raise his little brother, giving him his meals, his rest, teaching him. Now . . . I'm so very sorry I cannot be near you to embrace you and ease your pain, to wipe the tears from your eyes.

This evening the enemy attacked the hamlet after dark. Going down to the pitch-black shelter, I only thought of Nhieu. My tears are mixed with sweat. Oh, Nhieu, your third brother, your fourth sister,[148] and I will avenge you.

1 September 1969

The farewell to Tan has unsettled my heart with worries and yearnings. Our brother-sister bond has grown. I believe he holds a special love for me—a brotherly love, a revolutionist's love, but with the depth and warmth of two kindred souls.

This afternoon, flipping through his notebook, I find the brief letters I hastily wrote to him on pages torn from a notepad. I know Tan always burns or tears up letters after reading them. Keeping my letters shows that he reserves a corner in the page of his life for me.

Among the instructions he gave brother So[149] was the specific task of protecting me, of safeguarding an important Party's asset. Secretly, I smiled when I overheard him reminding So, "Remember, I'm counting on you."

I don't know whether brother So perceived Tan's big-brotherly concern for his little sister.

Oh, Fifth Brother, have a safe journey. I will welcome you back with the deep love of a little sister.

---

[148]Thuy meant that Thuan was Nhieu's third sibling. Nhieu's sister was younger than Thuan.

[149]Brother So was a member of the Party's governing board in Pho Van village.

3 September 1969

At 12:47 a.m., Uncle Ho[150] left us forever.

Oh, Uncle! Your children vow to fight and fulfill your wish, to persist in your endeavor: Liberate the South, secure independence and liberty for our nation.

We've suffered the most painful loss. Uncle Ho has passed away.

Oh, I don't cry, but my heart bleeds with indescribable grief. Oh, Uncle, why did you leave us when the endeavor is still unfinished! Our nation is not yet reunified. Our compatriots in the South haven't had a chance to welcome you, yet you have lain down to sleep forever. Oh, Uncle, from beyond, perhaps, you are not yet at peace to see that half of our nation is still submerged in fire and smoke, that the blood of the Vietnamese people is still flowing freely for our endeavor and yours.

Missing you, your children vow to fight to fulfill the common goal. Missing you, our tears have condensed into hatred for the American bandits.

Uncle of mine, uncle of the people of Vietnam, of the proletariat of the world, believe that you never die, your name and your mission live on forever!

4 September 1969

After a few days of being apart, Tan hands me a handwritten letter. I want to tell him so many things, but I cannot talk. I think he feels

---

[150]Ho Chi Minh was affectionately called *Bac Ho,* or "Uncle Ho," by the people of Vietnam.

the same. He is always surrounded by people and work! How can we find a day for just the two of us, Fifth Brother? Can we only share our confidences through letters and diaries? No, I won't accept that, Fifth Brother. There must be a day for you to tell me everything, brother.

13 September 1969

Young brother, distance and time only make me feel closer to you. I miss you more than ever. The day we meet again is far, like a faint dot of light in the night. I am a lone traveler on this dark road, looking toward that light, my heart withering with longing.

Do you know how I struggled to get you transferred closer to me? When I realized this wish was unachievable, I was crushed.

Among thousands of terrible worries is one thing I cannot forget: When can I see you? When can I live next to you as we did in the old days?

Don't fall, brother. Live, you must live so that one day I can hold you, cherish you with the noble love that I have for you, my young brother of the South.

The fighting goes on; you and I are soldiers standing at the front. Who knows what will happen, but let's believe as Simonov[151] believed, in the poem "Wait for Me":

Oh, little brother . . . wait for my return!
Wait for me forever, brother. . . .

---

[151]Konstantin Simonov (1915–1979) was a prominent Russian writer, poet, and playwright popular in Vietnam, known particularly for his poem "Wait for Me," written during World War II. The line "Wait for me; I will come back," is often quoted by the Vietnamese.

14 September 1969

I dream of things that have made indelible impressions on my mind.

I see myself returning to Hanoi after so many days away; I see Dad, Mom, and you . . . the young brother of the South, in Hanoi. I see you, Thuan. I am surprised by your stare—your eyes shining with pain. Oh, this must be the true picture of today's extremely perilous life.

These days I often feel lonely and cannot suppress the sadness pressing on my heart. The clinic has not been established.[152] I am still wandering from place to place. The handbasket is heavy, but my worries are much heavier.

23 September 1969

September is almost over. Time flies incredibly fast.

Autumn has stepped onto the golden rice fields. Harvest is supposed to be a joyful time, with the hard-earned abundance finally arriving after so many days of labor, but the American bandits and the traitors are threatening the fields. In the early morning, waves of ships disembark troops for the raid; artillery shells pound the fields by the rice shed. . . . Fear and hate have stained the joy of the harvest.

Suddenly I remember the movies and the songs glorifying the socialist societies, and I feel my heart twisting with the question: When, when can the South have Peace, Freedom, and Independence?

---

[152]This was the second clinic in the North Wing of Duc Pho where Thuy was assigned to tend the wounded.

Among all the letters from the South Wing, there isn't one from you. Folks tell me you're sick and depressed. Traces of you linger in my heart. It doesn't matter where I am or what I do, I cannot forget you. Oh! Is there any way I can share your burdens and sufferings, brother? I wish my young brother well so we can see each other again. I am sending you a hundred thousand loving thoughts from afar.

Do you hear me, my strange brother?

20 October 1969

It has been a very long time since I wrote in my diary.

Is it good for an introspective person not to meditate? No, I don't want to live like that, but work demands so much of me. Every day, another death among my comrades makes me forget my personal matters. But this diary is not only for my private life. It must also record the lives of my people and their innumerable sufferings, these folks of steel from this Southern land.

Eighth Brother Vinh died!

Oh, Vinh, I will never forget you, the simple and diligent peasant who loved his wife, children, friends, and comrades with an immense love. There were nights I was sound asleep when he crawled quietly into the bamboo brush and bailed water out of the shelter pail by pail, so that if I had to go into the shelter in the morning, I would not be too cold. Many times he gave me his dry shelter and took the flooded and uncomfortable one. . . .

Did you really die, brother Vinh?

No, you are still alive, my diligent brother. You are loved and admired.

21 October 1969

The situation is extremely tense.

At Mo Duc,[153] military vehicles plowed through the hamlets. The villagers fled. Many cadres perished, crushed in their shelters by the enemy's vehicles. . . .

Listening to my big brother telling the story, I could not help feeling worried. I can see in his eyes that he is even more worried about me. The closer I am to him, the more our bond strengthens, even though we rarely have the opportunity to exchange anything more than warm greetings, a few simple questions, or a bit of conversation about work. Others tell me he is very concerned for me, but how can I tell him my longings for him when I am far away, and how can I know he misses me just as much?

Oh, big brother Tan, you are so dear to me, but why do I still find you unfamiliar? Is there some kind of wall between us?

25 October 1969

It doesn't seem imaginable that some people with the most important responsibilities in the district work and live in this forsaken place—an empty, crumbling house with an artillery shelter. Fear of exposure keeps them from cleaning up the place. The garbage

---

[153]Mo Duc is the district headquarters of Mo Duc District in the province of Quang Ngai, north of Duc Pho.

and debris are left untouched. At night, a buzzing fog of mosquitoes descends on the place. Dirt and pebbles fall through the gaps
between the planks. It is difficult for anyone to sleep.

Du Quang was one of the most beautiful and rich hamlets in
Pho Quang village, a bountiful place on the Duc Pho sea. Now
Du Quang's abundance can only be found in its artillery shelters.
These structures are big and well constructed. The walls are made
of shiny, hefty logs salvaged from destroyed homes. Inside, thick
planks are laid to accommodate thirty to forty people.

Each evening after dinner, everyone moves toward the shelters in preparation for the enemy's attack: grenades launched from
the gunships, bullets fired from Vang Mountain . . . and artillery
shells. . . .

Life is reduced to the minimum.

A horde of dangers looms over me.

30 October 1969

The flood covers the fields and the lower sections of the hamlets
with an immense blanket of water.

The Americans have been here since yesterday morning. I've
been up since 4:00 a.m. today, preparing for the enemy's attack.
The torrential rain hasn't let up. At 7:00 a.m., the Americans begin
their mopping-up operation. We go down to the shelter, which is
built like an artillery shelter, fairly large but old. Two of the vents are
blocked.

Rather than having just the two of us, brother Ky and I, staying
in the shelter, I let Eighth Sister stay with us as well. (Although

nothing will happen if Ky and I are alone, I still feel awkward, concerned that people might misunderstand.) Over an hour later the water begins rising quickly in the shelter, reaching as high as my chest. It's unbearably cold. We don't know where the Americans are, but we decide to leave the shelter and hide in the bushes.

At noon, Tam and Di come with their guns and lead us away. There is no habitable shelter. All are flooded. We still have no idea where the Americans are. Everyone stays at Tam's house. We are all soaking wet and shivering, but I feel happy to be a part of the resistance, to be in this very scene. Smiles can still blossom on my comrades' pale lips.

By the fire, the radios and watches are laid out to dry.

1 November 1969

Crossing the highway at night—all my senses alert, every fiber in my body taut with tension. The flooded area is immense and the enemies are all over the highway, but we are not to be deterred. Brother Tan decides to go, so I also decide to go, no matter how difficult. My organization has only three people left, but because of unfavorable conditions we cannot all go. At 5:00 p.m., I follow brother Tan to the boat dock. The road goes through hamlets bulldozed by the enemy, everywhere a chaos of fallen trees and crushed houses. Here and there, a few abandoned homes survive. Frightened villagers have already fled from the raid, taking with them rice and cookware. The scene is so sad it almost makes me cry.

When we arrive at the dock, there is only one boat left for

fifteen people. We must decide to leave half of our group behind. Besides the scouts, there are only three other people going: brother Tan, Kinh, and me.

We go in silence, carefully stepping on the edge of the rice paddy, down the thorny trails. While we are crossing the drain under the highway, I imagine myself like Marius[154] walking in the sewers of Paris. I never feel afraid (it seems this has become my nature). Ahead of me, brother Tan often looks back and always finds me smiling at him and looking curiously at the bright lights mounted at the enemy's posts.

Oh, Fifth Brother, wherever I am, I want to be joyful and strong in my convictions. Crossing this road tonight, I am happy because I am facing these perils with you, because I have you leading me through dangers. . . .

We reach our destination at 11:00 p.m.

Farewell, brother Tan, have a safe trip and return soon, dearest brother.

5 November 1969

Incessant rain. I am in a house untouched by war, with a happy family, but its warmth cannot touch me. A hot meal before me, I think of others. Are you on a rainy and windy road, Fifth Brother? The cold wind blows through your thin shirt, you must be shivering. I wish my affection would cross the distance and warm your heart.

---

[154]A character in Victor Hugo's novel *Les Misérables.*

This same hour, on the far South Wing, where is my young brother in the land full of fire and smoke? In a flooded shelter or in a jungle? Each day away from you, the distance seems to grow longer. I am resigned to suppressing my yearning.

At this moment, how many families are homeless? Where do their gaunt children live?

Oh! Cruel American bandits, your crimes are piling up like a mountain. As long as I live, I vow to fight until my last drop of blood in this thousand-year vendetta.

12 November 1969

After three arduous months of wandering and struggling against the enemy, I return to the forest. My heart aches when I look back to the lowlands. The hamlets and villages that have been sheltering me are now under the enemy's stampede. They have leveled the land from Duc Phong to Portal Mountain. Standing at the tip of Hoi An,[155] one can see clear through to the beaches of My A!

Our agony!

The survivors are wandering through the devastation, homeless. They cannot leave their homeland, which has been rendered barren by the enemies' bulldozers. They cannot leave, for their hearts are bonded to the revolution—to their husbands and sons who are fighting this war. Each evening, wives steadfastly return to the turmoil to make meals for their husbands, and old mothers

---

[155]A hamlet of the Pho An village, Duc Pho District.

return from their hiding places by the river, their clothes thoroughly soaked, to feed their children.

23 November 1969

Today is Phuong's birthday.

Oh, little sister, I remember you and your birthday not because of the cold wind and drizzle blowing in from the north. No matter where I am, I always safeguard the happy memories of our family in my heart. I miss the Sundays, the wonderful birthday parties in our cozy house filled with celebrating friends.

Today is also a Sunday. What is my sister doing to commemorate our birthdays?[156] Surely, you remember me as well. In your joy, I know there is a part of you that misses your big sister. You cannot imagine what I am doing these days. Today in the morning, I went to work with a machete in hand; at noon, with a medical satchel on my shoulder, I followed two guides to tend an ill comrade. On the road, I met soldiers.[157] Hesitantly, I paused to visit with them, but I did not know what to say. They had broken bamboo shoots to eat.[158] I could tell from their pallor and thinness that they had been hungry and suffered from malaria for a long time.

This grandiose resistance is written with the blood and bones and youth of so many people.

You know this, don't you?

---

[156]Because Thuy's birthday was November 26 and her sister Phuong's birthday was November 23, they celebrated their birthdays together.

[157]The soldiers were from North Vietnam.

[158]The soldiers did not have rice, so they resorted to eating bamboo shoots.

26 November 1969

Another year of living, another year of fire and smoke on this dangerous battlefield of the South.

I wish you steady steps on this victorious road you have chosen, Thuy.

You are not sad when only the forest leaves murmur to you in the torrential rain.

You are not sad when the only celebration music you hear is the sound of the stream gushing down to the lowlands.

And you are not sad in this room where you are writing this page of your life, this tiny, dark underground shelter.

You will not be sad because when you reopen these pages years later, you will be proud of your youth.

Here, you do not have the cozy moments among friends gathered around a table, a vase of fragrant roses at the center.

Here, you do not have the happiness of strolling side by side with your lover on the empty road as the violet twilight fades behind the sunset. Here, you are without many things, but you are also self-sufficient.

So smile, Thuy. Be cheerful, Thuy, when the book of your life opens onto a new page full of victories and beauty.

29 November 1969

The construction of our clinic isn't finished, but we must move again.[159] A bastard has betrayed our location to the enemy. Others

---

[159]Having been unsuccessful in establishing a stable clinic location between April and November 1969, Thuy moved to the South Wing of Duc Pho District.

are hauling rucksacks onto the road once more to search for a new haven, but I go back to the South Wing.

Goodbye, North Wing. As I leave, I feel no attachment, only worries. The enemy is ravaging the north side of this district. I wish my comrades staying behind a strong will to stand firm in this fight to make this beautiful, abundant land calm and joyful again.

30 November 1969

Traveling is always dangerous, particularly in this war zone occupied by the Americans. Passing through Pho Nuon,[160] I see not a single shadow of life, the bare houses stripped to the bones, with half-burned columns standing like ghosts.

I don't know why I miss Fifth Brother. Is this your homeland? Why is your homeland so ravaged? In the deserted gardens, the deep violet hundred-day flowers[161] give me a feeling of restless regret and longing. I pick some flowers, not knowing what for, but I hold them awhile until the river crossing, when I release them to float down the river.

No, I will not forget you, my companion. I have these simple but remarkable memories.

1 December 1969

Coming back to Pho Cuong,[162] I'm anxious and happy to see friends and acquaintances. Pho Cuong is still as it was in the old

---

[160]Pho Nhon is a village in Duc Pho.

[161]A variety of chrysanthemum.

[162]Thuy fled to the Pho Cuong area in the Nui Dau mountain region.

days, populous and content. Folks welcome me warmly, showering me with affection.

It has always been like this. I always feel like a child returning from afar to live once again within the loving fold of her family.

2 December 1969

I see young brother again. I have imagined that the minute we met you would put your head in my arms and cry. I will be speechless if Nhieu is not in the old house when I step inside. But I don't know why we only smile happily when we meet. How am I to come back and live near you and feel your love? Those days living in the North Wing, I could hardly imagine a time when I would see your shining eyes again, could hardly imagine the moment I could hold your hands and touch your hair. That moment is today. There is also Thuong next to you. The three of us have lived many happy days together. The bonds of the revolutionists warm my heart. I no longer feel cold, despite chilling wind and rain settling over the hamlet.

I will be on the road again tomorrow. I promise to see you and other dear ones again, my young brother!

3 December 1969

The night is cold. The chilly northern wind blows in gusts, numbing me. Shivering, I run to your side. You put a sheet of parachute cloth over my shoulders, and you squeeze my hands. And I am warmed.

The time of departure is not yet here. I want to delay it a little, but time does not oblige me.

At a quarter to four in the morning, Thuong and I shoulder

our backpacks. My young brother sees me to the gathering place. The farewell moment I recognize in his shiny dark eyes—I say good-bye to him like kin.

When can I see you again?

Have the fire and smoke of war robbed me of my tears? Before, a sad movie could make me sob. Now I can bite my lips and stand here in silent farewell. The one who leaves, the one who stays behind, no one knows if any of us will survive after the parting.

Earlier this afternoon, standing at the grave of little brother Nhieu, I felt my heart being ripped apart, but tears didn't fall from my eyes in torrents. His grave lay by the side of the road. The flowers had not wilted. He died more than a hundred days ago, but it seemed as if he fell just yesterday. I lit incense for his grave. I choked and did not know what to say to him.

Oh, Nhieu! You died like a heroic soldier. Your life is a song for the lips of the living.

Oh, Nhieu! You died young, your life still verdant with beautiful dreams and blossoming love. Your dear ones and I can only promise to continue the fight to avenge you.

4 December 1969

I see Van again. We hug each other, and I am so moved to see my friend's teary eyes. I have returned into the arms of Second Sister, into the arms of brother Ky . . . into the arms of my dear comrades.

The happy days and nights in the little house compensate for the past perilous days.

Dang Thuy Tram in an eighth grade student photo, Hanoi, 1958. *Courtesy of the Tram family.*

Tram family during Tet, Hanoi, 1960. *Front row, left to right:* Hien Tram, Thuy Tram, cousin Ha, Grandfather, Kim Tram, Grandmother, Phuong Tram, cousin Long. *Courtesy of the Tram family.*

Class 8C, Chu Van An high school, Hanoi, 1958. Thuy is in the first row, fifth from the left. *Courtesy of the Tram family.*

Thuy (*left*) and Thanh Mai after winning the gold prize for a duet in a student festival, Hanoi, 1959. *Courtesy of the Tram family.*

Thuy in high school, Hanoi, 1959. *Courtesy of the Tram family.*

Thuy with girls from class 9C, Chu Van An high school, Hanoi, 1959. Thuy is in the back row, at right. *Courtesy of the Tram family.*

Thuy (*right*) and Phuong Tram, Hanoi, 1960. *Courtesy of Nguyen Tuan.*

Thuy with Youth Union members, class 10C, Chu Van An high school, Hanoi, 1961. *From left to right:* Dang Thuy Tram, Duong Duc Niem, Tran Duc Kiem, and Hoang Ngoc Kim. *Courtesy of the Tram family.*

Medical students after a visit to Chua Lang, a pagoda in a Hanoi suburb,1962. *Courtesy of the Tram family.*

Thuy's medical class helping a farmer in the fields, Thai Nguyen, 1962. *Courtesy of the Tram family.*

Thuy (*right*) with Do Thanh Tam visiting the Vietnam countryside as a medical student, Thai Nguyen, 1962. *Courtesy of the Tram family.*

Thuy in Reunification
Park, Hanoi, 1965.
Courtesy of Doan Que.

Thuy as a medical
student at Bach Mai
Hospital, 1965.
Courtesy of Doan Que.

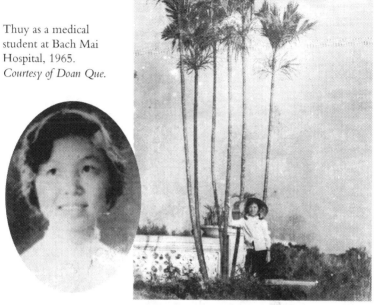

Medical students in Reunification Park, Hanoi, 1965. *Courtesy of the
Tram family.*

Thuy and Uncle Hien (Doan Que) before leaving for the South, Hanoi, 1966. *Courtesy of Doan Que.*

Thuy (*left*) and Phuong Tram, Hanoi, 1966. *Courtesy of Doan Que.*

Thuy with her family before she left for the South, Hanoi, 1966. *Front row, left to right:* Mother Tram, Khuong Bang Ngoc (M.'s sister). *Back row, left to right:* Bich Hanh (a close friend of Thuy's), Thuy Tram, Uncle Hien. *Courtesy of Doan Que.*

Thuy (*left*) with her mother, Hanoi, 1966. *Courtesy of Doan Que.*

Thuy (*left*) with Nguyen Thi Dung, Uncle Hien's wife, and Phuong Tram, Hanoi, 1966. *Courtesy of Doan Que.*

Thuy in Pho Cuong, Duc Pho District, 1968. *Courtesy of the Tram family.*

Thuy playing guitar in Pho Cuong,
Duc Pho District, 1968.
Courtesy of the Tram family.

Guerrillas in Nga Man
hamlet, Pho Cuong,
Duc Pho, 1970.
Photograph by Nguyen Gia.

Dang Thuy Tram's gravesite in Tu Liem Martyrs Cemetery, where her
remains were moved in 1981. *Courtesy of the Tram family.*

BOOK II

1970

Spring, The Year of the Dog[1]

Hold firmly the spirit of a communist, a spirit as clear as crystal, as hard as diamond, a spirit shining bright with a thousand halos of faith. A communist loves life dearly but can accept death just as lightly if necessary.

—HOANG VAN THU

---

[1] The Dog is one of the animals in the twelve-year cycle of the Chinese calendar.

31 December 1969

We move back to our old station on New Year's Eve. The farewell to acquaintances and dear ones at Pho Khanh leaves me with many unforgettable memories.

A month ago, I came back to Pho Khanh after two years. Van was the first friend to embrace me with tears in her eyes. My faithful friend loves me like kin. What can I do to reciprocate your love, Van?

Tonight we leave again, walking on the familiar trails full of tiger-tongue thorns. I am deep in thought. The fighting grows more vicious each day. Death is close. Just the other day, if I had been a few minutes late, I would have been dead or captured. We started to run when the enemy was less than twenty meters away. Fortunately, no comrade or wounded soldier was lost. But I lost my whole backpack.[2] The only thing I had left was a small handbag containing a box of special equipment and a radio. After a night sleeping in the jungle and a day climbing the mountain, we arrived at the place where the folks of Pho Khanh were staying. We lived there in their care, among families like Bon's and Truu's,

---

[2]During the attack, Thuy lost her entire backpack, which contained two diaries. She wrote about the incident in a letter to her mother.

people like Hon, Long, Ba, Duc. . . . They pampered me. There were Hoan, Tong, brother Xu . . . kind and thoughtful comrades.

When we left today, friends and dear ones walked with me a long way. When can I return here to cross windy An Khe Lake in a small boat?

Good-bye, dear Pho Phanh. Good-bye, Van, I promise to see you again one day.

1 January 1970

Another year of life, thirty isn't far off for me. In only a few more years, I will have become a seasoned and serious cadre. The thought leaves me with a fleeting sadness. My youth has flashed by in a whirl of fire and smoke. War has robbed my youth of happiness and love.

Who doesn't cherish the spring? Who doesn't want to keep her bright eyes and lips full of youth? But . . . in this era, the young people in their twenties must put away their rightful dreams of happiness. . . .

The dreams now are of the American bandits' defeat, and Independence and Freedom for the nation. Only when those dreams are fulfilled will I be able to have my own wishes. Like other adolescents, I have gone to the front. Our youths have vanished in the explosions of bombs, the sounds of bullets. My youth has been soaked with the sweat, tears, blood, and bones of the living and the dead. My youth has been tempered in the perilous trials of the battlefields. Day and night, my youth has burned hot with the fire of hatred.

And something else . . . is it true that the spring of youth is brighter with the color of hopes and dreams flashing in someone's eyes looking at me?

Dark with sleepless nights, those eyes still look at me with joy and excitement.

And there is also another shiny pair of eyes with long lashes that always turns to me with immense affection and trust.

And yet another set of cunning eyes—a girlfriend—looking at me with total understanding and trust.

Oh, Thuy! Isn't that a happiness that only you can have? Be joyful, keep dreams and hopes intact in your heart, and let the green color of youth shine forever in your eyes and in your smile, Thuy!

2 January 1970

I am a grownup, but why do I behave like a sullen little student who turns away when there remain so many things to be said? I am still a spoiled little girl in the emotional cradle. The affections of dear ones have made a soft cradle and lulled me into the dream of youth.

When will I stop asking life to pamper me? When will I know enough to be patient like the caring mothers, like the capable wives who bear all the hardships for the happiness of their families?

I can't be like that.

For my dear ones, I can bear material deprivation and physical hardships, but I must have priority in intellectual matters!

3 January 1970

We had said good-bye on this same road long ago, when you accompanied me to the foot of the mountain. Now you are here again, still simmering with love and burdened with worries. You can only utter a few brittle phrases to me before we bid each other good-bye.

The night is as dark as ink. Rain pours down in torrents. I cannot remember the road, so I stray for a long while. I do not blame you, but I feel strangely sorry for myself. I know that during the meeting your thoughts follow me, my every shaking step down the muddy road. How sad . . . young brother! Why can't we walk together as before?

Oh, brother, whatever happens, polish your affection, keep it as bright as a gem. Don't leave any stain on it. Let us be courageous. Let us be calm and clear-minded in all situations. Protect our pure, noble love until we die.

January 1970

Seeing you again in the crowd, I cannot say a thing to you. Oh, Fifth Brother, love can never be whole on this fiery battlefield, can it?

I remember the farewell that night. You held my hand, but you could only say, "While you stay home, little sister, beware." Looking into your eyes, I knew what you meant.

Farewell again. Oh, why always farewells, worries, and longings? Go, my dear brother, my dear comrade who has led me through perilous roads. I hope when I see you again I can share with you my confidence, the confidence of a little sister to whom you have given a unique brotherly love.

6 January 1970

Too much work, too many tasks have given me a headache. Maybe something else caused it as well. Something disquieting. A precious stone in my hand falls to the ground. Even if I pick it up, it's no longer shiny. Although it is not broken, it's scratched, damaged. Oh, Thuy, how sad it is!

Please, Thuy, follow M.'s advice: "Persevere, never relent, not for one minute. A lapse of vigilance will cause a regrettable chain reaction." Sharpen the qualities that make a good Party member.

Thuy, your life is a book; the lines written there are as beautiful as the lyrics of little songs. Please, write worthy lines.

Promise your conscience that you will keep safe the high values of a Party member, of an educated person in a socialist society.

"Hold firmly the spirit of a communist, a spirit as clear as crystal, shining bright with a thousand halos of faith . . ."

M. once asked me, "Am I Vu Khiem and are you Huong Giang, Thuy?"[3]

How can I answer that question now? The war has robbed me of all my dreams of love. I neither want nor am capable of thinking about love, because this life does not allow it.

---

[3] Vu Kiem and Huong Giang are characters in the play *The Call of the Front* by Tran Quan Anh. The play was particularly popular among students and young people in the North in the first few years of the war.

So go, M., follow the call of the battlefield, and I will stay behind, but I will also give my all to the efforts at the front. I promise to talk about it later on our reunion day, dear comrade!

7 January 1970

Here I stand in a mountain forest, in the skirling wind;
Rain weaves a thick blanket over the trees.
Hearing the northeastern winter wind moan,
I suddenly feel a gnawing pain in my heart.
Oh, dear ones afar, do you know my thoughts this cold
    afternoon?

This afternoon . . .

You there, walking between the lines of trees
On the immense road of the nation's heart,
You there, walking in the middle of Reunification Park[4]
Gazing at palm shadows, thinking of the South,
Passionate visions of loved ones,
Arriving suddenly at the heart of Hanoi.
Just like some festive nights on the Lake of the Returning
    Sword,[5]
Shoulder to shoulder, we happily welcomed Spring.

---

[4]A park in the center of Hanoi.

[5]Legend has it that Le Loi (1384–1433), the emperor of Vietnam and founder of the Le Dynasty, had a magic sword of extraordinary power, similar to King Arthur's Excalibur. There are many versions of the story, but most agree that after having defeated the Chinese with his magical

This afternoon . . .

On top of Truong Son
The Soldier of Liberation marches to the battlefront.
Oh, beloved, what do you think, looking at the Southern
   Range?
The waves of Sa Huynh Sea[6] are still salted with
   yearnings,
Still calling, murmuring day and night,
Still waiting for you to return with glorious victories.
Promise me we will hold hands to welcome Spring
In happiness, the day our nation finds peace.

This afternoon . . .

In a cottage in the familiar hamlet,
What thoughts bring tears to my eyes?
My yet youthful hair has endured much sun and rain
But still, noble and true love has not faded in the heart.
In the long nights on the road to duties
My restless heart returned to the old road
Where we parted
With love-laden farewells.
Do you know that even if I die

---

sword, Le Loi was out in a boat on a lake in Hanoi when a large turtle surfaced, snatched his sword from him, and dove back into the lake. Le Loi realized that the gods had lent him his special sword to defeat the Chinese, and now that Vietnam was free, the gods had taken it back. So he named the lake Hoan Kiem, or "Lake of the Returning Sword."

[6]Sa Huynh is a coastal village in Duc Pho, Quang Ngai Province.

For our nation's future freedom
My dream and love remain forever true?

This afternoon . . .

I see those dark eyes have not rested the night,
You, with a thousand thoughts, sigh softly, weighted with
*   worries.*
Worry for our countrymen, our comrades, our brothers,
Oh, my dear ones, who suffered when bombs fell.
This afternoon I fly back to reunite,
Kiss my loved ones, eyes brimming,
Tears falling with this salt of love.
We cross the perilous road, over rivers and jungles,
Eyes steadfast on the future, we disregard the brambles, the
*   thorns,*
And, you know, love gives me long wings.

8 January 1970

Party's review. I tremble at a comrade's mistakes. Never, Thuy! Never let the sub-branch of the Party hold a review meeting like that for you.

This afternoon, sitting on the trestle bed in the operating room, I suddenly remember Lien. She lived and died here. Lien's grave is on the hill. I have not visited it, but each time I come to this room

I remember her. Life is so short, but each passing day must be a worthy day.

Don't let anyone tell the story of our lives with criticism.

9 January 1970

I'm missing you—who are you? A dear one, a comrade, a beloved young brother or a stranger. What should I say here?

A cluster of long-life chrysanthemums
A branch of Ochna flowers
Compete in blossoming bright colors
In the golden morning light.

What will life be like, Thuy?

10 January 1970

Party Sub-Branch General Meeting. I'm one of the three board members elected. I'm surprised to be here because I haven't been a member of the Party for very long. But, in this revolution, many people grew up like Phu Dong Thien Vuong,[7] and I'm one of them. The road still has countless perils. I wish you steady steps in your advancement, Thuy. Flatten all opposing forces. Be as worthy as the most loyal member.

---

[7]According to a Vietnamese myth, a child from Phu Dong village grew up extraordinarily fast to defeat Chinese invaders, and then he went up a mountain and disappeared. In recognition of his heroism, people called him Phu Dong Thien Vuong, "Heavenly King of Phu Dong."

12 January 1970

For me, these last few days by your side have been heavy with thoughts. It's hard for me not to talk, but then again, what is there to talk about? What needs to be said has been said. Oh, what's there to say when life is counted by seconds, by minutes? I don't want to think far ahead. I only want to talk about things before our eyes. That is, each minute of our lives must be a proud minute. There are innumerable hardships in front of us.

I hope you will safeguard our affection, let it be a source of motivation, something for you to lean on, young brother.

13 January 1970

So M. is gone! I could never have guessed that things would turn out the way they have. Eight years ago, under the shady line of trees, I bade farewell to M., who was leaving for the South, without a single tear or a promise to keep my heart faithful to him for the next five years. Then I, too, went to the South, following the call of the nation and of love. I saw M. again. . . . Everyone thought nothing could compare to the happiness of our reunion. But life has so many ironies. When we were apart, I called out to M. in silence, every second, every minute. But when we met, I let my pride overcome my love.

M. is not mine alone. Of course, he saves his highest love for the Party and for the people, but if there is too little love left for me, then . . . my fervent heart cannot be satisfied. I do not demand that we must be together, that we must marry, but I only hope that our love is still bright and vibrant despite the bombs and bullets, the fire and smoke of this war. But this is something M. cannot do, and so I must force my heart to forget all the loving things that have nourished it for more than ten years now.

As M. says, "Thuy has a passionate and faithful love and so much pride."

In the last three years the two of us have only met twice. M. and I both feel sad when we think about love.

Whose fault is it? Mine or M.'s? Nobody can answer that. Everyone gives us his thoughts. Some advise me not to continue loving a person who does not deserve my love. Others, who understand M., urge me to forget pride so the two of us can be together again. We only smile at their suggestions. No one understands our love. And only our own ideas can resolve this matter.

Now M. has left without seeing me. In a letter he sent back, he writes, "Being in love does not require us to be near each other. Whether we are in the South or the North, whether we are near each other or a thousand miles apart in rain, sun, and burning sand . . . everywhere, I am still the one who truly loves you after eight years, and the one who will love you truly for many more years to come. Let us live as the two dearest people on earth. The right to decide belongs entirely to you. . . ."

This pledge is acceptable. Here, I will also reserve my life totally for the fight and the assignments—there can be no other love. And there, M. probably cannot truly love anyone else when he thinks of me.

Life has set us on this road, and we must try to go forward. When we see each other again, only then will we talk about the future.

I wish you, M., my beloved comrade, a safe departure. I send you a hundred thousand warm thoughts, these longings from your friend and comrade.

15 January 1970

Afternoon rain in Dong Ram.

I come back to Dong Ram. I left this place temporarily on 28 April 1969, when the enemy attacked the clinic. Returning today and seeing the foundations of collapsed houses, the burned tree trunks, the disarray, I feel my heart aching with sorrows.

This place holds so many sad and joyful memories of my revolutionary life. Here, in this place, I was accepted under the flag of the Party after such a long, difficult struggle.

This place has trained me from a freshly graduated student to a leading cadre with some achievements.

In this place, a high and immense love between a sister and a brother began. It was a relationship that supported each of my steps through this thorn-filled path of life.

At this stream, one afternoon, I had waited for my young brother. Under this tree, I had sat with him after my absence . . . so many memories churning in my mind. . . . The enemy had robbed me of two diaries. Although I lost those precious pages, I still have the most valuable book—my mind. It will record everything in this life.

19 January 1970

Thank you, dear comrade. You came to me with the sincere affection of a kinsman. Life is so complicated. I don't know how to live in a way that satisfies everybody. Like you said, it's natural. I have never been pessimistic when faced with obstacles. As I have said many times, life is a colorful painting; besides the red of victory and the green of dreams, there are also the black of death and the gray of cold and deceit. But I still love life, the life of the revolutionary, earnest in love, passionate in conviction, in one's strength.

Dear Fifth Brother, do you believe me? Believe your little sister, brother?

21 January 1970

Watching my own behavior, I realize I have been unreasonably frustrated the past few days. . . . Where did those frustrations come from? Other people also feel as uncomfortable as I do.

Oh, Thuy, you cannot be like that. Be strict with yourself. Train yourself to know how to yield to people below you, to become a good and kind little sister, a responsible cadre, to understand public opinion and to place common interests above all. You must be humble. Your prestige comes from the respect and affection of the people, not from your own assessment.

I hope that you will conquer these weaknesses.

22 January 1970

It's a desolate afternoon in Hoc Bau. The specialty training is over. The class from Pho Cuong has just departed, leaving behind a silent, empty house without shadows of people. Coming back to this bleakness, I cannot hide my sadness. Is it because of your yearnings, Thuy? Surely some of them are also sad to leave this place. Oh! My heart is always brimming with emotions.

24 January 1970

The moon shines as brightly as a mirror. The dew chills the night. The cold cuts the skin like razors. The thin parachute cloth isn't warm enough. I am shivering. The cold keeps me awake. Perhaps my heart is brimming with so much love that I cannot rest—in my ears the warm breaths of my beloved comrades.

This struggle is fraught with perils. Yesterday on the road, the enemy's bootprints were still fresh in the mud next to a comrade's body. Electrical wires[8] from the enemy's mines were still strung all over the road. We went through Deo Ai Pass immediately after the enemies came through. They would return in a short while. . . .

Death is so near and simple. What makes our lives surge forth so strongly? Is it the love between our people? Is it because the hope for tomorrow still burns hot in our hearts? Is that it, my beloved comrade?

28 January 1970

Joy and hope shine from those eyes. When did hope awaken?

Since those blinding sunny days of summer when fire and bullets lit up the sky?

---

[8]Thuy is describing the M18A1 claymore mine, a U.S. antipersonnel mine. The mine, a curved block mounted on a tripod, was detonated via an electrical wire, and directed its shrapnel (700 steel ball bearings) outward in a fan or semicircular arc two meters high and fifty meters wide. The claymore mine was intended to protect areas from enemy infiltration and was used to defend bunkers, bridges, and checkpoints along roads. Along roads where children were traveling to school or guarding water buffalo, they would trip mines that had not been deactivated, and be killed or lose limbs. U.S. soldiers in the field developed an unorthodox use for the mines; they would remove the explosive charge, which produced an intense heat, and use it as a field stove to cook C-rations.

Since those dim moonlit nights on assignment?

Since those perilous minutes when death came near? . . .

Oh, Thuy, the girl full of will and reason, do you have enough strength to stifle that hope?

He nurtures a hope against all odds, a notion as wild as growing an orchid in a desert of date palms. No! The orchid must live in a porcelain pot. It would die in the desert. We must understand that, and we must plant it where it can live. Perhaps there will come a time when we can change nature, change our fortunes, and make flowers grow in the desert. But the time has not come, at least not for me.

29 January 1970

Baby Nga died. She was singing just the other day, her head tilting to one side: "Con Co has a racing fish that is a stone crab that lies in the crevice that has eight fins. . . ."

Nga was born in the forested mountains of Gia Lai. Her mother had been holding her with one hand as she cleared the jungle with a machete with the other hand. For four years she raised Nga while studying and working on public assignments. Every Vietnamese woman endured hardships, but probably few suffered as much as Mrs. Su. Married and pregnant . . . delivered the baby and then raised the child alone, but she never received one word of encouragement from her husband. Because of a misunderstanding, her husband did not accept Nga.

For four hard years, she studied while raising her daughter. Time was not kind to her. She aged much before her time, but her road was also complete. She became a pharmacist, a Party member, the mother of the sweetest and most obedient daughter, and a gentle wife who could please her husband. She came back to the plains to see her husband again and spent a few happy days with him. Less than a month after she returned, baby Nga died.

Baby Nga died of pneumonia without treatment. The enemy never relented with their endless raids. Nobody knew Nga was sick, so no one visited Mrs. Su's house near the enemy's outpost.

Nga died. I feel so much for Nga and her mother (but Mrs. Su has misunderstood and treats me badly). That's because of the war, too! Otherwise, why can such a banal illness kill a baby like Nga?

1 February 1970

These things are nothing, but they're like thorns pricking me. You must protect your honor, Thuy. Hone your character so you won't regret looking back on the road you have traveled.

Let's see if I am a person worthy of M.'s and others' trust. The road crosses so many abysses. A little negligence will be enough to make me lose my footing. Be alert, beware.

2 February 1970

These departing steps are heavy with hatred. There will always be departures like this as long as there are American imperialists. It's a moonless night. I want to see each comrade's face clearly, but the lamplight reaches only a few. I stand looking at you, beloved young brother. I hope you will be vigilant. I will stay awake and wait for your return. I cannot extinguish the worries in my heart. Oh, who can understand how valuable each second, each minute of life can be? One minute alive is one minute to serve the revolution. I want to be carefree, but it's not possible. How can I be carefree when my comrades' blood still drenches the road?

3 February 1970

What is this sense of desolation that permeates the air and even me? Is it my dear one's wide-open eyes, full of regrets for the failure in his assignment? Is it the destitution of these kind families during the Tet holidays?

I can't understand it. I only feel sad. Whose sadness is it that presses so heavily upon my heart?

Tet doesn't mean a thing.

Oh, Thuy, are you pessimistic? Does spring no longer come to your heart? It's sunny and dry, but still cold just like the other year. I see the sunlight warming the bed of mustard greens, but I am cold without the presence of my dearest one.

Now . . . eight years have passed.

6 February 1970

New Year's Eve.

The fourth New Year's Eve away from home. New Year's Eve living far away from dear ones. Oh, Hanoi, tonight people are together, shoulder to shoulder by the Lake of the Returning Sword.

The Turtle Tower[9] is glittering with lights. But I know the joy of my Hanoi cannot be complete. How can Hanoi's joy be full when so many of its people are far from home, their hearts still bleeding? Tonight every heart must be filled with longings. And here we have flowers, Tet rice cakes,[10] songs, and music, but my heart has only longings.

This is my first time celebrating Tet in the lowlands. Oh, Thuy, can't the affections of the folks of the plains warm your heart? A smile on the lips is not a smile in the heart!

No, be joyful with the spring, Thuy, love today, love each second, each minute of life.

7 February 1970

A night in spring, drizzle wets my hair. The night is dark. In the middle of the hamlet, the sandy road glows white in the starlight. With worry, I bid farewell to my young brother. The situation will get very tense. I am going away and leaving behind much hardship.

Oh, brother, will we be able to meet again? Oh, the detestable war! It only brings us suffering, doesn't it, brother? I know I was wrong when I said I could not hope to see Mom and Dad again someday. You scolded me for being pessimistic, but I was only being realistic.

---

[9]The Turtle Tower is a small tower built in the middle of Hoan Kiem Lake (Lake of the Returning Sword).

[10]Tet rice cakes are a traditional food for the New Year's holiday. Made of "sticky rice" with a mung bean and pork center, the square rice cakes are wrapped and steamed in banana leaves.

Farewell, my young brother. I will certainly see you again. I will kiss your dear eyes.

15 February 1970

The days living next to you, I am happy.

I am happy to feel us growing closer in our brother-sister relationship each day. I believe in you as I believe in myself. And this belief helps me advance, helps me crush all obstacles and take control of my life. I am so happy to have you lead me across the dangerous places, to have you take care of me in every small thing, to have you teach me with the kindness of a big brother toward his little sister. Even with your responsibility as a district secretary, you still support me, a comrade new to Party duties. You give me friendship in this life-and-death struggle.

Keep it whole forever, "consistently pure" Fifth Brother.[11]

18 February 1970

More than ever, I wish young brother could go to A.[12] If you go, I will lose a support, a source of consolation and encouragement. I will lose a person who protects me in every respect. . . . But I still wish it for your future. The situation where you are has been very tense the last few days. I cannot stay calm when I hear the tanks rumbling down there. Salvos of explosions come to me like hammers striking my head.

Oh, young brother, beware.

---

[11]From correspondence.

[12]"A" means North Vietnam.

19 February 1970

I'm so happy to see my young brother again. It's like reliving the days when the clinic was still at Dong Ram.

You come up from the plains with a heart burning with longing, but when we see each other, both of us are so calm as to seem indifferent. Why is that, young brother?

Tonight, sitting at the organization meeting in the middle of the forest, I feel your gaze upon me, I feel your affection and joy.

Oh! Our relationship is so passionate.

Hearing that his mother died and his father was seriously injured and carried away by the enemy, Tam cried silently many times. What can I say to console him? The words coming from the bottom of my heart make him weep even more. I cannot bear to scold him like the others. They want to stop the sad scene by mentioning their own misfortunes. I have witnessed this so many times these last few years, and yet my heart still shivers with empathy, and I'm almost afraid to see it again. Thuan also comes to console Tam. He looks at me, and I know he wants to say, *This was exactly my situation a year ago, and it has happened again—do you understand, sister?*

Oh, affection for you also comes from the same tears. I feel for your loss and I bring my sisterly love to warm you.

20 February 1970

I keep looking at that girl. Her body is strong and proportionate. She has big eyes and honey-rich skin. Her long hair falls down the

length of her back. There is a sadness lingering in her smile. I wonder what happened. Did she have that sad smile because she lost
her true love, or did the sad smile make her lose her true love? I
feel for her the way a person sitting in a warm room might feel for
someone walking in the cold. She must continue her walk, for she
hasn't arrived at her destination. It seems she is jealous of me. Her
jealousy is not that of a girl whose lover has eyes for another. She
envies me because I have won the affection of a particular person.
Although this affection is not love, it has a strange weight.

Life is like that, so complex. Even when you want to live simply, it's impossible.

21 February 1970

I come close to death once more. Several gunships and HU-1As
bombard us for over an hour. One of the points of impact is
roughly ten meters from us. Fire and shrapnel fly everywhere. Ear-
piercing explosions. My comrades and I sit in the shelter without
knowing when a bullet will strike us. Death seems palpable. But
then it all passes. The enemy's attack isn't precise. They leave after
the raid. We hurriedly vacate the area.

Departing, I look back at the beautiful trees and our construction.[13] I feel a cutting pain in my heart. For almost two months,
more than ten people put all their strength and enthusiasm into
building this place. During the cold and rainy days, when the steep
mountain road was as slippery as grease, our clothes soaked, we still

---

[13]Thuy is not clear in her journal entries whether the clinic was permanently or temporarily
abandoned. Although the clinic staff had cultivated two thousand manioc plants, they abandoned
this food source to move to a more remote location.

laughed and sang as we carried lumber on our shoulders to build the structure. At noon, no one wanted to rest. We decorated our place right after lunch . . . so much effort. . . . Now the fruit of our labor is no more than the little crabs' sand caves on the beach. . . . What is there to say? When can the wounded soldiers have a place to lie down? When can we return to an orderly operation like before? I feel so much for my comrades who have struggled these past days. . . .

22 *February 1970*

There are nights we sleep in the forest with the green canopy for our roof. The Lady of the Moon playfully shines through the leaves. She shines on me. Her smiling eyes seem to sympathize with me, a cadre in hardship.

I wake up in the middle of the night, staring restlessly at the moon and thinking—three years on the battlefield, I have matured. Lying here, I worry for the wounded soldiers who don't have a place to be treated. I have all the worries of a person responsible to the Party. As for myself . . . there is nothing to worry about. I have volunteered, I have offered my entire youth to the nation. Even if I must sacrifice my life, there is nothing to regret. You must be worthy of each day you are still alive, Thuy. Honor is an invaluable gem. Do not let anyone tread on it, no matter who he is, or how powerful.

24 *February 1970*

I want to reproach you. Why did you behave like that? With you, I only want you to avoid making the same mistakes you made with

Le and Mit. Think carefully, young brother, you who are so passionate and headstrong.

Tonight the three of us, sister and brothers, confide in each
other. I am deeply moved. Perhaps this is our last meeting. We all
understand it as true, as an apparent truth. What can I say, young
brothers? I only can say that despite bombs and fire, I will faithfully
safeguard our relationships. Our road has so many pitfalls and thorns,
and so do our relationships. Don't think that my reprimands and
my anger mean that I do not love you. It is because I love you immensely and want you to have complete happiness. Reading your
diary, I know you love me more than anyone else. But why are you
hiding things from me? I am so angry with you. I want to be generous and forgive your shortcomings, but I can't do it. I had to say
it aloud. If you place our relationship above everything else, then
things will be fine. Otherwise . . . it's up to you. I always keep a
little bit of a bourgeois girl's pride, so I cannot do otherwise.

25 February 1970

The job of leadership is very complex and immensely difficult.
How can I please everyone? Oh, Thuy, in whatever situation, you
must firmly uphold the following:

- Work correctly with principle.
- Hold high public opinions.
- Learn from people with humility.
- Sympathize with each comrade.

You are still inexperienced. Try to learn and train yourself. . . .

The conversation with sister Xu also allows me to understand some issues. I need to be more careful with each word, each act, because there are picky and jealous people. That's life.

But what is that for? We should live together with true love. This fight has a thousand perils. Life and death are so close together. What's the sense in counting the small things?

26 February 1970

I feel strangely sorry for Chin. This wounded soldier is very young. With a bandaged arm and shaky steps, he must leave the clinic. Chin can still laugh and sing, but I know he is very tired. Who knows that this young boy is a hero, a slayer of American soldiers, an excellent guerrilla from Pho Cuong, the best village in the district? My affection is sudden and keen, although when he leaves I merely urge him to beware and try to exercise the arm for fast recovery. And I look lovingly at him. OK, go, young brother, I wish you a quick recovery to return to your unit to fight.

27 February 1970

Life is indeed a painting, with thousands of colors and textures. I am like a painter fresh out of school, stepping into a complex reality. Before me lies a long range of high, dark blue mountains with strands of white clouds spreading lightly on their slopes. The mountains are raked and scarred by bombs, the raw red earth like open wounds. Since I stepped onto this steep road full of perils, lined with trees withered by poison, parched beneath a burning sun, I have encountered cool streams with flowers and fragrant blossoms. . . . And the faces I met on the road have been kindly. There are shiny eyes, looking at me with affection. There are inquiring eyes, trying to understand me. And there are also crafty eyes here, trying to cheat me with jealous looks and fake smiles. . . .

Oh, Thuy! Choose wisely, be wise and calm. You are not young. I wish you knew how to act. Don't squander your trust. Don't be stingy. You must know how to place your personal interests below those of the Party cooperative. Why is Thuan able to attract support from everyone? Like me, he has been a leader growing up from the instantaneous outgrowth movement. (Thuan became a Party member in November '68 and a secretary of the Party branch in June '69.) Isn't it because he is capable of doing the things I've mentioned?

On this road of life, everyone stumbles, everyone has imperfections. I am not afraid of imperfections. I must overcome what is wrong and try to expand on what is right. Do not follow the public, do not be autocratic or bureaucratic, do not be afraid of disappointment, do not abandon principle. Before doing something, I must weigh its merits carefully. I am an actor on a stage with many eyes looking at me. I can do it. That's obvious because I am an actress. They only praise me when I am exceptionally good (I am not capable of that yet). If I am deficient in my role, they will criticize, criticize mercilessly: With a performance like that, she wants to be an actress, very bad, and so on and on. . . .

It's a natural thing. If my position were different, no one would say anything. They would understand and feel sorry for me, a girl away from home, a fragile girl who knew only happiness since childhood, but must now endure so many hardships. But things are different now. They say, "Ah! That girl is my leader, are her contributions to the revolution only half as much as mine? After so many years of dealing with death on the battlefield of the South, I am under her command! . . ."

No! Comrades, I work only for the Revolution. The Party assigns me important responsibilities only because it wants to maximize my capability and strength for the service of the common good. I am honored by the Party's trust, but I am not arrogant. I am well equipped with knowledge gained in the classroom, but I know it cannot compare with real-world experience! My three-year experience here cannot equal the experience of comrades who have served ten, twenty years on the battlefield. So come to me with the warmth of comrades who have sacrificed for the nation's freedom, come to me as friends who are far from home, as lonely souls who have adopted the revolutionist family as a pillar of support in this life. Advise and help me to become an effective member to serve the Party. For my part, I know myself, and I know what I must do. I'm aware of my capability. I tell myself I must learn humility from the people around me.

28 February 1970

Today, I suddenly miss sister Hai. Her letter, filled with loving confidences, touches my heart. Oh, sister Hai, I will never forget the afternoon in that fierce summer when I saw you leave with tears and sweat running down your face. I could not go with you, but I kept following you all the way to Ong Thuong hamlet. Then you went away. . . . Each time when I come home and see mother[14] and young brother Lai, my heart stirs with memories of you. Lai has already grown up. He is half a head taller than me. His eyes and mouth are like yours. He loves me very much. A revolutionist's sentiment has strange strength. It binds people who understand each other with an invisible but unbreakable cord. I never intend to ask mother for anything, never take advantage of her affection for material gains. You and our other dear friends are like that too, sister. But there are people who could not understand this kind of love.

Oh, sister, do you know how much I miss you?

1 *March* 1970

There are nights when my dreams become very vivid and real. Why? Have certain things become deeply imprinted in my mind? Is it because I'm living here in a place laden with memories?

The room in the heavy afternoon rain of October '68. A beautiful moonlit night on the bench. A meeting of the Party branch. Washing my clothes in the stream on sunny mornings. An operation, the hot, tired breath of my assistant standing next to me. A late night coming back after my rounds in the patients' ward. The silent farewells where neither those who left nor those who stayed knew what to say. . . .

These are the hours, these are the days I have spent here. It's the same everywhere I look, every place carries such deep memories.

Why is that, Thuy?

I know my sentiments are just like those of Jean Valjean toward

---

[14]Tram is referring to Tran thi Khiem. Tram called Khiem's mother as her own because she thought of Khiem as her sister.

Cosette. It's the sentiment of a father toward his daughter, a big brother toward his little sister, and above all, it's the consummate love, consolation, and hope of life. I am not like Jean Valjean because I am not lonely. Though, in some regards, we are similar, Valjean and I. That orphan girl thrived with the old man's love, but no matter how much she loved him, she must also have her own life—Marius will come to her.[15] That's it. But, oh, Thuy! Don't be like Jean Valjean, you are different. Life welcomes you with affectionate arms, leading you toward advancement and maturity. You have many dear ones, not like Jean, who had only Cosette. So, Thuy, you should not be selfish. For Jean Valjean, Cosette was his entire life. As for me, I do not need that. Why do I need that? I should try to be a person in control of her emotions.

5 March 1970

I feel very restless and yet pensive each time I make contact with that girl. Is she and can she be . . . the worthy life-companion of my young brother? I am debating a similar issue for myself. I trust Fifth Brother as I trust myself. He says that she is, so I must believe him. What can we say now, my big brother? Can this girl promise my young brother's happiness?

Thinking of him, I feel very sad. His feelings for me are still very sincere, but not as fervent as they once were. Isn't that true, young brother? In the past, when you came back from assignment in the middle of the night, or when you survived a severe fever, or when you'd just escaped the enemy, all you could think about was

---

[15]Cosette, Jean Valjean, and Marius are all characters in *Les Misérables*.

me. . . . Now it's no longer like that. Isn't it true that the war has hardened your heart the way it did M.'s?

Last night I dreamed of dear ones from both the North and the South. Among the loving images of Dad and Mom was a familiar face with shiny black eyes looking at me anxiously. . . .

7 March 1970

Away from Pho Cuong for the entire month, I have a strange, mixed feeling, half missing and loving, half blaming that dear homeland. I have so many bonds there, the familiar roads with inundated trenches, the bamboo clusters by the side of the roads, with their tops tattered by artillery shells. There are the smiles of the young guerrillas, the cordial greetings—"Second Sister"—from everyone. There are also sorrows and people I disliked, but . . . in the end, all of that is because of me. Try to live worthily. Nurture and protect your honor. Of course, you cannot live to satisfy everyone, but you must deal with your weaknesses.

8 March 1970

I don't admit to forgiving my young brother, but . . . why is that, Thuy?

Is it because your gaunt face, with its shadows of sadness and sleepless nights, has made me feel sorry for you? Is it because your voice is full of regrets during our unfinished conversation? Is it because life is so fragile?

This afternoon, an errant bullet fired by the soldiers under the bridge struck a girl in front of her house, piercing her abdomen.

This same afternoon, a shirt hung out to dry caught the eyes of the bastards on a gunship and resulted in a raid with all kinds of bombardments, killing nine, wounding twelve, with four more missing, only two escaped. If it hadn't been for your task of tailoring a shirt and my presence, you would have hidden at that place. . . .

Are these the reasons why I forgive you? No, that's not possible, Thuy! I act on my responsibility as a big sister. I overlook everything to nurture the love you and Cuc have for each other, but forgiving your shortcomings in our relationship is not possible.

Don't let affection make me relax. Leniency will lead to the destruction of the noble sentiment that you and I have promised to protect all our lives. Don't let love command my life. I must be like Pavel, like the Gadfly, or like my M. Definitely, be like that, Thuy! My comrade, do you understand that?

26 March 1970

There are memorable moments in a revolutionist's life.

Silently, I listen to that dear comrade breathing softly on my hair. And his slender fingers caress the calluses on my palm. I feel his fingers pause and squeeze my hand tenderly. Every day, a "deep, pure, immense" love becomes greener in my soul. I protect it with care, determined to keep it intact, whatever happens. Oh, my dear comrade! Is it because life around us burns so intensely with hatred that our fellowship in this struggle binds us to this holy love? Although today's life is still full of dangers and hardships, let's hold hands and go forth steadily to stamp flat all obstacles. . . . We met each other on the road for

people who share the same ideal. Our love is completely different from the romantic sensation between boys and girls, but it
also has miraculous strength that gives us joy and hope. It helps
us forget the sufferings all around us. It is the fire that warms
my heart, a fervent heart that needs to be nurtured with pure
and rightful sentiments.

27 March 1970

It's life at the base. Naturally, I'm a part of it. At 4:00 a.m.,
we wake up to eat and get on the road with a *ruot nghe* bag.[16] We
arrive at our destination, where we intend to stay. We don't know
until we get there that the place has just suffered a ferocious
bombardment. The whole forest has been ripped apart, trees down
everywhere, houses leaning askew, walls and roofs nearly gone.
Silently, I put down the backpack and look at everyone. My
comrades smile, but I can see in their eyes that they are worried . . . preparation for the Uprising is coming, what will we do
then?

Tonight it rains, drumming on the backpacks, the pots and
pans, and leaving melancholic notes in the air. I look at him. He
is pale and thin, too many long nights without sleep, too much
work and worry. My big brother, no matter how much I love
you, I have no way to protect your health. My own conditions do
not allow me to do anything. Let it be so, brother. You probably
understand me.

---

[16]A sack used for carrying rice. When filled, the sack resembled a sausage, long enough to be
wrapped or tied around the body.

29 March 1970

The enemy threatens the clinic. HU-1As and scout planes circle above the trees. The grenades, short-range rockets, and machine guns are deafening. Artillery bombardment from Chop Mountain falls near our shelter. Huge shrapnel shatters a tree trunk in the middle of the operating room. A question reverberates in my mind: If the enemy comes, how can we move the injured in time? Earlier, Thanh and brother Xuat went out on observation assignments. They haven't returned. I hear small-arms fire and see helicopters landing in that direction, but I don't know if anyone got hurt.

Worries are pressing heavily on my heart. Suddenly I remember your words to me: "Why come to the South to suffer? It's happier out there, but you didn't want to be there!" Did you reproach me? I know you did not scold me. You asked because you felt sorry for me. You were the third person to ask that question. No, it is through suffering that we understand the value of the revolutionists. He who stands firm in fire and boiling water will be like steel. As Nikolai Ostrovsky said, "Steel tempered in fire and ice will be harder, will overcome all trials. . . ."

Tonight the forest is silent, suffused with a strange lightness. Here I cautiously listen to events and follow the enemy's movements. Over there, you are probably following each of my steps.

29 March 1970

For the first time, I dig a grave to bury a comrade. The shovel hits a rock, and sparks fly like the flame of hatred in my heart. Yesterday, returning from an observation assignment, Thanh was shot right at the stream on the path that led to my house. The enemy wounded brother Xuat and then they landed to take him away. His torn pants were left at the site. . . . In less than three months, the organization has lost three people!

The grave is not yet finished, but people are already carrying Thanh back. A day has passed, but blood still seeps from his body, soaking the wrapping sheet red. I cannot see his face clearly, but only a pair of closed eyes and pale face. Alive, Thanh had weaknesses that I didn't like, but now, shoveling earth to cover his body, I cannot hold my tears. That's the way it is. Try to love and care for one another when we are still alive, but when we are dead, crying is only tears on a lifeless mound of earth.

30 March 1970

Sadness, immense sadness. Oh, my dear ones! What can I say so that you can understand my heart? My road is so perilous, this road of a female student going out to lead. What makes me different from others? My way of life? My sentimental life, a life rich with meditation and a touch of the bourgeois? . . . What is all this? This is precisely what differentiates me from other people. I feel pain when others around me are jealous and critical. They think that they are good, that they are modest. . . . Oh, Thuy, be calm and firm, admit mistakes, and correct them at the roots. Don't be sad. You already understand life. Save those tears until you can lean your head on the shoulders of your dear ones. They will understand your heart, and they will ease your pain with their boundless compassion. Smile, Thuy.

Oh, you, the student with three years of service on the battle-field full of fire and smoke. Walking through these thorns of life, your feet have hardened with calluses. Go courageously, go steadily, socialist girl in this land of the South.

1 April 1970

Anniversary of my acceptance to the Youth Union. Ten years have passed, from a teenager to a woman, you have become a cadre seasoned in fire and smoke, Thuy. I am not being arrogant, but I have kept my vow to the Youth Union flag since that first year.

The long, pensive nights. Oh, Thuy, you must be more severe with yourself. Don't let the question stab at your heart: Why doesn't anyone understand you? Instead ask: Why don't you let them understand you? There are petty, jealous people and there are people who cannot talk. So let's behave as they do. Don't cry, Thuy. Save your tears for the day you see your dear ones.

Late at night, I'm lying next to my comrades. They are sound asleep, their breaths are even. Outside, artillery shells explode all over the sky. Oh, my comrades, we breathe the same air on this fiery, smoky battlefield. Let's love and care for one another. Death is so close now. Why be jealous and quarrel?

5 April 1970

Is this loneliness making me long for my dear big brother so much? This afternoon, Cuc left to go back to serve at the organization. Suddenly, sadness and longings threaten to overwhelm me. Why is life so complicated, and why am I so sentimental? Why? Because I've been like this since I was a child.

Listening to sister Hanh's opinions, I feel strangely sad. There are those who live with such narrow views, incapable of seeing sincerity and brightness. They see only materialistic things, only sex! Oh, how detestable.

My big brother, is it true as you've said: "Our relationship will last forever, no matter how time and distance change"—meaning we will live righteously, simply, we will overcome the barbs and garbage obstructing our path? I will also live as you do. I will carry out my exact promise to you.

9 April 1970

A strange dream, it combined images of the days when I lived in the North and the South. There were visions of my colleagues and me in our white blouses, sitting in the ophthalmology class,[17] microscopes in front of us. And I saw the beautiful house where the district commissioner's staff worked, a place where I came and went as freely as though it were an ordinary house. I met you there in well-ironed clothes. You were the dear big brother who took care of every little thing for me. I also met his wife. She still had her sadness and her simple clothes. . . .

Oh, is this a vision of the future?

Tomorrow, when there is peace once more, I will return to

---

[17]Thuy had been accepted for advanced medical study in surgical ophthalmology, but declined in order to work in South Vietnam as a physician.

the old school and rejoice with all the people who have endured this struggle with me. We will be happy together in this new peaceful world.

10 April 1970

The dream becomes real, but reality is only a part of the dream! It seems I don't feel happy when the thing I wish for becomes true. Why is that? Am I a revisionist?

22 April 1970

It has been a very long time since I read this treasured letter from my young brother. A shadow of sadness lingers in your letter because you think I do not love you. In fact, I always keep your dear image in my heart, but as I've said to you, though love can be expressed brilliantly, there are times when it must be kept in secret and silence because one should not or cannot express it.

Do you know that, young brother? You are mine and mine alone.

27 April 1970

Thuong is captured!!!

Oh, he is his mother's only son. She is old, and she has struggled all her life to raise him. All her hopes and dreams have been vested in him since he was born . . . but now! Oh, my young brother, who is gentle, unassuming, insightful, and mature in this struggle, has fallen into the bloody hands of the enemy.

Suddenly I remember the last night I saw Thuong. That night, the pale moonlight spilled down on his solemn face as he held my hand and whispered, "I probably won't see you again, sister." I scolded him: "Why do you say such an unreal thing?" But he replied in his low voice, "It's very real, sister. It's normal for a revolutionary to sacrifice his life. I have survived the last ten years on incredible luck. I can't be lucky forever."

Oh, why did you predict such a horrible thing? My heart bled today when I heard you had fallen into the bandits' hands. Is this the end? I can no longer see the simple, gentle brother from Pho Hiep, can I?

Now grief cannot be expressed by tears, but only by one's determination to extract revenge, by clenching our teeth and raising our heads to continue on the perilous road.

28 April 1970

I am supposed to be happy because all my dearest friends from this southern land are around me. It is rare when big brother, his wife, and two young siblings, mother and I[18] . . . can be together. But the joy was like a brief summer breeze. When big brother and big sister depart, leaving behind two young siblings and me, I cannot sleep. There is sorrow in my heart. Oh, the war still continues. Still, so many losses and sufferings.

---

[18]Thuy is referring to her adopted brother's family.

29 April 1970

What can I say to you, young brother? Listening to you, I cannot stop the tears coming to my eyes. Indeed, you say that if you fall, there is no one to continue your bloodline. With this thought, you want to get married. But, oh, brother, what will become of your love and your happiness when you both must face the countless difficulties awaiting you? Loving you, I want you to have a secure happiness; I don't want you to become tormented by the question of whether you should follow your own idea, or others', or mine. Holding your hand, I want to place in it all my trust and affection, but I stay silent because I really do not know how to use my trust and love for you in the most appropriate way.

3 May 1970

The situation at Pho Cuong has turned precarious again.

Tanks rumbled into the area just as I left. Enemy aircraft dropped troops right where I lived. Thuy, Lien, Hung, Loi, all were captured. . . . What happened to my young brother?

Worry leaves me utterly exhausted. Oh, if there is a way to protect you, I will pay whatever price. Kim comes over. Seeing her teary eyes, I understood her heart. Oh, Kim, you are not a perfect girl, but I love you because you love my young brother dearly. Like me, you can do nothing, even though worries are burning your heart from within. You can only resign yourself to watching the enemy stomping on our homeland and threatening our loved ones.

Oh, little sister, there is no other way.

5 May 1970

War spreads in Indochina. The mad dog Nixon has foolishly enlarged the fighting.[19] We will have to cope with a more terrible reality. But I have sworn with my comrades: even if I must die, I will fight to the end. . . .

Oh! Hatred is bruising my liver, blackening my gut. Why are there such terrible, cruel people who want to use our blood to water their tree of gold?

So much and still not enough for their greedy pockets, so much and still not enough to satisfy the foolish desire of the bloodthirsty devils.

7 May 1970

We commemorate the sixteenth anniversary of the victory at Dien Bien Phu, that historic victory which broke the French colonialist invaders.

Sixteen years have passed, but blood still flows and bones still break in this country. The South has been at war for twenty-five years. Oh, my country! Twenty-five years immersed in fire and bullets, we are still strong. We will persevere and be courageous and hold our heads high and take the offensive. Blood soaks each of our steps on this road of struggles! Is there any country on earth that has suffered as much as ours? And are there any people who have fought as courageously, persistently, and tirelessly as we have?

---

[19]President Nixon announced on April 30, 1970, that the United States was invading Cambodia, an event that sparked widespread domestic antiwar protests in the United States.

This afternoon, everyone goes down to the plains. I don't know if they will make it through. The enemy shells the road with their artillery. Perhaps my comrades are still at Xoi slope. . . . My heart burns with choking worries, sadness, and hatred.

13 May 1970

Nghia was injured in a combat operation. One of his arms was broken.

In the past when I was away from my young brother, there were times I wished I were near him—if he were injured, I could take care of him. . . . Now it's real. (My M. had wished "to have the hands of doctor Thuy" care for him, but it was not possible.)

Being away from me for a long time, Nghia has become thin and much older than his twenty-three years. The pain in his arm causes him to groan. All this stirs my heart. I want to take him in my arms and ease his pain, but I don't. Not everyone can understand this pure love. People will make deductions. Nghia's belongings are meager, one set of underwear on his body, one pair of shorts Thuan gave him . . . a notebook for recording work, in which I find the farewell notes I wrote in 1967 when I left to go back to the base. The notebook is wrapped carefully in plastic. My heart stirs when I know that he takes my writings with him on all the roads to battle. Young brother, let's keep our relationship forever dear, like the days when we used to live together in the homeland Pho Hiep.

In fact, in the past days, some things have faded from our beautiful bond because we did not know how to preserve them. Was that your mistake or mine?

19 May 1970

I receive a letter from Mom. . . . Oh, Mom, each line in your letter, each word is full of love, like blood flowing to nourish my distraught heart. Oh, does anyone understand how much I want to go back and live with my family, even if it is just for a moment? I have known this since the moment I first stepped on the truck that took me down the road to bombs and bullets. But I still went away, following ideals. In the last three years, on each road I traveled down, in the deafening cacophonies of a thousand battles, there was always a sweet and intense sound in my heart that was louder than bombs and thunder. It was the voice of the dear North, of Mom, Dad, sisters, all. From the rustling of the row of ironwood trees on Dai La Street, from the lapping sounds of the Red River to the intricate sounds of the capital, all still reverberate in me incessantly.

So many times in my dreams, I have returned to Hanoi, to the loving arms of Mom and Dad, to the clear laughter of my young sisters, and to the brilliant light of the city. Having been away from home three years, five years, or however long, I am certain that my longing will not change. Others can go away for money or fame, but only the Party can make me leave my family.

I am still a soldier in this struggle. The enemy comes, firing intensely. Still, I smile and calmly go into the shelter. The enemy attacks our base. Even the nights on evasion maneuvers when I must sleep in the forest, I keep my smile. I keep it blooming even when gunships and HU-1As launch rockets down on my head. . . . And yet, when I think of my family, of the dear ones in both parts of the country, I crumble. My heart aches, and tears fill my eyes.

Is it because my heart has been baked in the fire of war, but is still weak? Is it acceptable for a revolutionary to be like this? I remember Lenin's words, "A revolutionary has the most sentimental heart." This is me.

22 *May 1970*

I come back for the District Youth Union meeting. Being among young people makes me cheerful. The situation is extremely dangerous, with the constant threat of attack. The enemy has stealthily moved closer to our meeting place without our knowledge. Focused on cutting trees and laughing, we only know their presence when a highlander charges in to warn us that the enemy is right by our side. We evade their sweeping operation. Fortunately, we handle the emergency well, otherwise they would have killed us with their gunships, artillery, and infantry. Even in the madness, we are still able to be cheerful. The smiles have not vanished from these young faces. Each night in the small house, we hang our hammocks close together and tell jokes. It's hard to be serious with all the laughter. . . .

What makes me cheerful? Is it the affection of everyone, of Phuong, Ton, Hao, Hang, Minh, brother Ky . . . and of this whole happy family?

24 *May 1970*

Big brother is going away on a long trip, but in a way it seems he has already left. Even as I look at him, I feel he is already gone.

He is already distant in space and time, and what else? I tell him if he is not gone by the time I leave, I will only say a brief good-bye and not another word.

I am furious with him. The day we ran back to inform him of the enemy's situation and asked his advice for a resolution for the youth organization, he reprimanded Ky for not being alert enough and because the whole District Union Board lacked a clear mind. . . . I was so angry with him. Right then, I urged Ky to leave. I did not say good-bye to anyone, and I didn't say anything else to him. That night he sent Cuc to tell me to go back to his place to sleep, but I never went back. He knew me; my pride was hurt! For several days I didn't return to his place. Even in the meeting, I kept silent . . . until now.

We are about to say farewell. If he is not going, I will definitely leave in silence. But until now my deep affection for him has not allowed me do that. I have to write a short letter with these thoughts.

Before going, he leaves a letter that stirs my heart. It turns out he also understands me.

But why, big brother? Why did you not say that I am your biggest concern? Before we met again, you said you missed me immensely, but when I arrived, you kept quiet. Why? Oh, dear big brother, you are so close and yet so far. I understand you totally and yet not totally (and you also still ponder the same about yourself!). Why is that, big brother?

25 May 1970

Big brother's observations of me:

- Good awareness of the revolution, clear and correct idealistic motivation.
- Considerable progress in many areas.

- Needs to do more scientific research.
- Certain bourgeois characteristics still remain.

2 June 1970

A common accident in war: a series of bombs falls exactly on my clinic, killing five people in the patients' ward at once. Everything, all that we've worked for, is consumed by fire and smoke! After the explosions, there is silence, a terrible silence. I think everyone must be dead. A few minutes pass, and suddenly sister Lanh shouts, "Everyone in Mr. Chanh's room is dead!" We all run outside. Oh, what devastation! The area has been blasted bare, a vast hole in the forest, trees downed in every direction, houses flattened or knocked askew, tattered clothes blown up into the tree branches. . . . By the time we dig up Nien and Buoi, dusk has fallen.

In the house, Thanh, who had an intestinal operation yesterday, suffers more serious wounds today. He is in agony. Thanh looks at each of us and says in shallow gasps, "Live, fight to avenge me. I'm dying."

Oh, my courageous comrade! Your last words are our vow, the vow of those still alive. We must fight to the end and take revenge for the dead.

Nearly a whole night without sleep, we go at first light. Leaving again. "The resistance against the Americans to save the country may last longer, our countrymen may have to sacrifice more property and lives, but we will surely win. . . ."

Oh, Uncle Ho, your words still reverberate in my ears, and at this moment they mask the sound of bombs and bullets, they are in my heart everywhere I go.

4 June 1970

Why can't we be at ease when our feelings are still miraculously pure and fresh? After all the times when death was so close to everyone, I am fortunate to see big brother and young brothers again. Instead of rushing into each other's arms and weeping with joy, we all held back, looking at each other without saying a word!

Oh, my dear big brother, my precious young brothers . . . why is it that we can't embrace each other, cherish each other in a good and fitting manner?

The Revolution of the South! Many acts of heroism, many historic events, but also so much complexity and garbage in this society. It's easy to understand because with all our counter-the-Americans-save-the-country endeavors, we cannot yet focus our strength to rebuild our society, to teach our people how to behave and live in a civilized manner.

6 June 1970

Sitting here on a summer afternoon and reading Van's letter, I am touched by her rough lines. Oh, sister Van, be proud that we are loyal despite the distance, despite the terrible perils. Do you know that your lovely words have kept me company down all the dangerous roads and brought a warming light to my heart? Some might say we are close because of our positions and our family's wealth . . . but position and money mean nothing. Here, in this place, they are too far and strange to us.

Van is an ordinary girl in a war-torn country. She is different from other girls in that she has the sacrificing spirit of the revolution. She has the courage to abandon a life of comfort and struggle alongside her countrymen in a land of bombs and bullets. Another difference is that Van is compassionate and friendly. Look at how she loves me. Van understands you, Thuy. She loves you and supports you in all that you do.

With Van, I am neither a doctor nor a high-ranking cadre. I am only an ordinary comrade—like her, a girl who dares to leave a life of comfort to go to the South and join the fight. Reciprocating Van's affection, I come to her with my open heart.

That's it, Van. On this perilous road, we lean on each other to walk. We will be proud of our friendship. Hold it with care, my dear friend Van!

10 June 1970

Why am I so sad this afternoon? Is it because I cannot see big brother before he leaves? Farewell once more. A farewell in this war, in all its destruction, could mean forever. Who knows if we will ever meet again? You are leaving in silence, aren't you, my dear big brother?

But this sadness is from Mom's letter. In her brief letter she tries to hide her suffering and longing, but her pain emanates from the few words she wrote without deliberation. Dear Mom, I understand your wilting heart is grieving for me, for my struggle in this terrible war. In my letters to you, I've told you a mere fraction of the dangers my comrades and I face, but you're still so very worried. If you know what we endure during the dangerous days,

what will you say? Dear Mom, if your daughter has to fall for tomorrow's victory, cry just a little. But be proud because your child
has lived a good life. Everyone dies only once.

Of course, I have always wished to come back to live with
Mom and Dad in the North and be embraced by so much love.

12 June 1970

I harbor intense wishes and longings in my heart. What do I wish
for? I wish for people to come back to reinforce the clinic so we
can handle the heavy responsibilities of the coming days. I hope
that my young brother returns at the end of the month, all my dear
ones. . . . And my biggest wish is for Peace and Independence so I
can return to live within the circle of Mom's arms.

Somehow my heart is heavy with yearning these past few
days. . . . Each night I dream of the North . . . each day I hope
and wait. . . . Oh, Thuy! The road still has many hardships. You
must continue on that perilous road. Persevere and be more
patient, Thuy.

14 June 1970

Sunday, it is clear and cool after the rain. The trees are brilliantly
green. In the house, a vase of fresh flowers just cut from the garden
this morning. In the middle of the room, beautiful sunflowers cast
intricate shadows on the shiny wooden table. The turntable is
playing a familiar song, *The Blue Danube*. . . . Voices and laughter
of visiting friends. . . .

Oh, that is but a dream—a daydream!

This morning is also a Sunday, fresh after a rain. The air is calm. If not for the sky-tearing roar of aircraft, this morning would be no different from my daydream. My place has just suffered another bombardment. The afternoon before yesterday, two observation planes circled for a long time and then launched rockets. . . . The explosions sent everyone running to the shelter. Hearing the bomb blasts above my head, I thought they were dropping bombs on the hillside in front of us. When the enemy left after four waves of bombardments, we were surprised to find that the bombs had struck not more than twenty meters from us. The entire area was denuded of trees. Plastic sheets covering the houses were shredded and scattered, flying everywhere. Shrapnel had cut beams and columns. Dirt filled the shelter! Fortunately, no one was injured. We all concurred that the location had been exposed.[20] We immediately began to find another place to build a structure and move.

All the healthy people went out, leaving behind five seriously wounded and non-ambulatory soldiers to be cared for by four female staff.

Yesterday it was pouring rain. We covered the floor with plastic sheets, but the water still came in and flooded the building. Everyone was thoroughly soaked. All day long we collected water dripping from the leaks and tossed it outside. The injured sat shivering, completely soaked.

---

[20]Thuy realized that they should abandon this clinic in the Nai Sang Mountains and relocate. However, given the small staff and the comparatively large number of seriously injured patients, it was not clear that it would be possible to move. U.S. military documents confirm that on June 14, 1970, a civilian intelligence source reported the existence of a "VC dispensary [clinic], 30 medics and 1 doctor." In Thuy's captured Vietnamese medical journal, she says that "members of the clinic are looking for a new location to construct a new clinic."

Looking at the scene, I laughed as my eyes brimmed with tears. Sister Lanh asked me, "Does anyone know about our situation?"

Who knows? Many people may have an idea but probably not a clear one. And likewise, I also cannot imagine any situation worse than ours in this drastic resistance. It is impossible to finish writing about life and death, and perhaps not everything should be told. My letters never tell my dear ones of all the hardships I have endured. Why make them worry even more than they are doing now? Thuan, my young brother, has brushed against death so many times. Suffering has imprinted his face deeply, the wrinkles making him look older than his years. Yet whenever he writes to me, his letters are always full of concerns for me, reminders for me to be more careful. And he says, "As for me, I am fine as usual!" I have learned that attitude from him.

Something presses heavily on my heart. What is it? Worry for the clinic? Is it this precarious situation, our vulnerability to the enemy's attack? Leave the wounded behind and run if the enemy comes? If they bombard our location again, what else is there to do besides sit in the shelter and wait and take our chances? The longing, the wish to be consoled by dear ones . . . all this settles on my heart. My soul is as full, as tumultuous, as a river after days of torrential rain.

Yesterday, in the ravaged scene after the bombardment, people departed, loaded with their belongings. Brother Dat gazed at me and asked half seriously, half jokingly, "Does anyone know about this situation? If peace is won, considerations must certainly be given to people who went through this." I felt a stab in my heart. I endured this not because I wanted to be considered. Is there anyone who understands my burning wish?

I said to brother Dat, "Oh, I don't need any consideration or recognition. My wish is for peace so I can return to Mom and Dad. That's all!"

Indeed, I do not think of the happiness of my youth, do not wish to be passionately in love at this time. I only wish to be re-united with my family. That's all. And nothing other than serving the Party and the Class.[21]

16 June 1970

My heart stirs as I read Boi's diary. He is a young student from Phu Xuyen in Ha Tay.[22] His feelings and secrets are the same as mine. We are living in extreme days. The clinic has been attacked, and the enemy is continuing to put tremendous pressure on us with all types of aircraft. The roar of an aircraft is enough to make me as tense as a taut guitar string.

There is no other solution than to stay with the wounded sol-diers. It is laughable that the commissioner for the clinic dare not stay with us. He refuses to stay with me. That's what it is: "Gold tested by fire, Will tested by danger."[23] I have resigned myself to bear this situation. What else is there to say?

These days, I miss the North intensely. Looking at the over-cast sky, I remember the afternoons I bicycled with my friends, riding leisurely through the nursery, the bright rows of pansies blooming like butterflies on the ground, the fragrant roses. . . . I

---

[21]Thuy is referring to the working class.

[22]Ha Tay is an area west of Hanoi.

[23]A popular Vietnamese saying.

also remember the willow-herb in the botanical garden—the flowers Phuong used to take home for display. Oh, the distant North, when will I come back?

17 June 1970

Today there are no scout planes circling over us. The air is calm. Once in a while, waves of HU-1As rise to hover above the hills. The enemy is certainly nearby. There are only three women here, with five non-ambulatory wounded soldiers. If the enemy comes, there is nothing we can do but run! Is that acceptable? Everyone agrees that in such circumstances, there is no other way. But will I have the heart to do it? . . . Nien, the injured young soldier, tells us sincerely: "Be calm, sisters. Run if the enemy comes. We will stay and fight them to the death!"

Nien is only nineteen years old. He is a commando, a very handsome boy with a full face, a high nose, and big eyes with thick lashes. When he is in pain, he turns to me with tears in his eyes.

Nien was injured in action. The wound caused secondary bleeding in the tibia. I had just operated on his leg three or four days ago, then the bombs fell on the clinic. A broken beam in the shelter crushed Nien's leg right at the old wound. For the past twelve days, I worried that his leg would bleed again. If that happened, it would be very difficult to save him. Today that danger has passed, but if the enemy comes . . .

Are you going to die, Nien? My heart hurts as if it has been cut open. I don't know what to say and what to do to protect the wounded soldiers whom we have tended with all our efforts for so many hard days.

18 June 1970

Dusk falls, the light dying slowly behind the distant range. The roaring of jet fighters and scout planes has ceased. The forest in the evening is terrifyingly quiet. Not a single bird chirps.[24] Not a human voice. There is only the murmur of the stream and the song from a transistor radio. I don't notice the song title. I am caught in the melody, as smooth as a rice field in the evening fog. Suddenly I forget everything, forget the heavy mood that has settled on me for the past few days.

Since this morning, except for the meal, the three of us each sat in a corner, staring intently toward the forest, searching for the enemy's approach. I never left my observation post, but my mind strayed to the day of reunion. I will come back to take good care of my dear family. I will value each minute, each second of the peace, because only by living here have I learned the value of life. Oh! Life traded with blood and bones, with the young lives of so many. So many lives have ended so that others can prosper.

Oh, the North, do you fully understand the heart of the South?

20 June 1970

Still no one comes. It has been almost ten days since the second bombardment. People left with a promise to come back quickly

---

[24]The bombs and chemical defoliants used during the war decimated the bird populations of Vietnam. Many Vietnamese commented on the eerie quiet, and on how sad they felt in the absence of birdsong.

and get us out of this dangerous area. We suspect that spies pointed out our location.

Since then, those of us who stay behind count each second, each minute. From 6:00 a.m. to noon, noon to evening . . . one day, two days . . . then nine days have passed, and they have not come back! Questions whirl around in our minds. Why? Why haven't they come back? Is something wrong? It is impossible that they have the heartlessness to leave us in this situation, isn't it?

No one answers us. We ask each other, frustrated and angry. Then we laugh, laugh as our eyes fill with tears.

Today there is only enough rice left for an evening meal. We cannot sit and watch the wounded soldiers go hungry. But if one of us goes out, there is no guarantee that she will be safe or that she can come back. There are too many dangers on the road. And if two of us go, leaving one behind, what can she do alone if something happens? Even without thinking about the remote possibilities, this rain in front of us is difficult enough. If it starts pouring in earnest, how can one person manage? She can't cover the shelter in advance because of the danger of being spotted by airplanes. Still, in the end, two of us must go.

Sister Lanh and Xang leave, and I stand there looking at them, pants rolled up to their thighs, wading through the stream, my eyes blurry with tears. . . .

Suddenly I recall a line from a poem:

Now immense sea and sky
Oh, uncle, do you understand this child's heart. . . .

No, I am no longer a child. I have grown up. I have passed trials of peril, but somehow, at this moment, I yearn deeply for Mom's caring hand. Even the hand of a dear one or that of an acquaintance would be enough.

Come to me, squeeze my hand, know my loneliness, and give me the love, the strength to prevail on the perilous road before me.

On the morning of June 22, 1970, soldiers from a company of the Amer-ical Division[25] heard the sound of "a radio playing VN music and voices of people talking" while out on patrol. Later that day, the 2nd Platoon spot-ted four people moving toward them down a jungle trail. One of them was Dr. Dang Thuy Tram, dressed in black pants and a black blouse, and wearing Ho Chi Minh sandals. The Americans opened fire, killing Thuy and a young NVA soldier named Boi. "The other two evaded off the trail and were lost by the element," according to the after-action report. Discov-ered among Thuy's possessions were a Sony radio, a rice ledger, a medical notebook with drawings of the wounds she treated, bottles of Novocain, bandages, poems written to an NVA captain along with his photograph—and this diary.

---

[25]D Company of the 4th Battalion, 21st Infantry.

A N O T E o n t h e T y p e

This book is set in Bembo, an old-style serif font based on typeface cut by Francesco Griffo for Aldus Manutius's printing of *De Aetna* in 1495. Today's version of Bembo was designed by Stanley Morison for the Monotype Corporation in 1929. Bembo is noted for its classic, well-proportioned letterforms and is widely used because of its readabilty.

The illustration on the title page is of a hand-cut paper bookmark found in Dang Thuy Tram's diary. The bookmark, along with the original diaries, is part of The Vietnam Project archive at Texas Tech University.

Printed in the United States
by Baker & Taylor Publisher Services